ENDORSEMENTS

Kathy Rogers shows us that real peace comes when we stop grasping for control and place our lives fully in God's hands. I have been deeply impacted by Kathy—her story is a beautiful reminder that surrender makes space for hope.

Jordan Montgomery
USA Today Best-Selling Author, Keynote
Speaker, Performance Coach Owner of
Montgomery Companies

There is a joy that transcends life's circumstances. It's rare to find someone who knows and lives in this stunning reality. Through heartbreaking loss and grief, I've watched Kathy discover it, and live in it, to the glory of God. This book will show you how to live with joy, regardless of what circumstances come your way.

Dr. Jeff Warren
Pastor, Park Cities Baptist Church

Kathy's story is a breathtaking testament to faith, surrender, and the resilience of the human spirit. Through unimaginable loss, she invites us to see life through a divine lens—one that captures God's light even in our darkest moments. Her honesty and hope remind us that grief and gratitude can coexist, and that peace truly is possible when we trust the One who holds it all. This book will meet you in your pain and lead you toward profound perspective and joy. Kathy doesn't just talk about faith—she lives it.

Ashley Smith
Speaker & NFL Manager of Player
Engagement

Look for Good is relatable and perspective-changing on so many levels. From the life-altering to the smaller, yet significant, moments, each is an opportunity to see and experience God. His transforming love takes Kathy's story of unimaginable events and reveals the importance of the lens we choose to interpret those moments. Your lens is a choice. The beauty of this story lies in one of its many lessons—that no moment is without meaning. Every event in our lives is an opportunity to see and hear from God. Allow God to transform your life through this book.

Bob Brooks
Host of the Prudent Money Radio Show

This book is made to be shared and discussed! Kathy Rogers doesn't shy away from pain, but neither does she let grief have the last word. Instead, she offers the antidote we all need in today's anxious, negative world—a lens of hope, faith, and compassion that comes only from God himself. Her story lightened my heart and strengthened my perspective, reminding me that if Kathy can choose to laugh, love, and trust God after all she's endured, then surely I can find that same courage in my own circumstances. This is a gift of a book for anyone seeking to rediscover joy during life's hardest seasons.

Ryan Minton
2X Best-Selling Author, Keynote
Speaker, and Leadership & Customer
Experience Expert

Few people can speak of grief, gratitude, and joy with such clarity as Kathy Rogers. Her lived experience makes her words both credible and compelling. This is a book for every season: whether you are walking through heartbreak, savoring a moment of celebration, or simply longing for meaning and purpose. Kathy Rogers has lived through the unthinkable, yet her words radiate hope, and this book will strengthen your faith and resilience.

Jon Gordon
18X Best-Selling Author of The One
Truth and The Carpenter

Look for Good is a beautiful reminder that God is with us in the midst of our pain and that His goodness is still all around us. Kathy doesn't shy away from sorrow. She shows that hope and healing come when we choose to see through God's lens of love. Her story reflects what we witness at One Bridge—when we trust God with our pain, He brings light out of darkness and joy out of mourning.

Brandon & Carol Syler
Founders of One Bridge

Through her powerful testimony, Kathy Rogers demonstrates that sorrow and joy are not opposites but companions on the journey of faith. Her story gives us permission to weep, laugh, and give thanks all at once.

Amberly Lago
USA Today Best-Selling Author, TEDx
Speaker, Coach, Podcast Host

LOOK FOR
GOOD

LOOK FOR
GOOD

Discovering God in Grief,
Celebration and the Every Days.

KATHY ROGERS

LOOK FOR GOOD
Discovering God in Grief, Celebration, and the Every Days

Copyright © 2025 by Kathy Rogers

All Scripture quotations in this text are taken from the Holy Bible, New Living Translation (NLT), copyright © 1996, 2004, 2015 by Tyndale House Foundation.

Cover Design by Jaclynn Braden
Interior Layout and Design by Alice Briggs
Editorial Team: Hallie Knox, Ginny Glass, Marcie Taylor

ISBNs:
E-book: 979-8-89165-364-1
Paperback: 979-8-89165-365-8
Hardcover: 979-8-89165-366-5

Published by:
Gordon Publishing

GORDON
PUBLISHING

*For the generations of faithful family members who embodied
God's love and helped me discover his presence in my life.*

CONTENTS

INTRODUCTION

W HEN I TELL people that I'm a breast cancer survivor, they usually overflow with well wishes and happy, genuine exclamations of "Praise God!"

To which I reply, "Yes, absolutely. Praise God!" My cancer was caught and eradicated (relatively quickly) about eight years ago now. The experience changed my world forever, and I am *so* grateful to be alive.

As the chitchat continues, I mention that, within a twelve-month period, both my mother and my daughter were taken by the same disease, facilitated by our shared BRCA2 gene. My mother lost her five-year battle with metastatic ovarian cancer in February of 2023. Not long afterward, Elayna—a wife, a mother, my dear twenty-nine-year-old daughter—was diagnosed with metastatic breast cancer, and she went to be with Jesus just six months later.

That usually turns the tide of the conversation. Reactions range from shock and sadness to complete awkwardness. Often, I find myself comforting whoever I'm speaking to, sharing a perspective on the story that may surprise them even more: a perspective of hope and gratitude.

That dissonance, between their reaction and mine, is why I needed to write this book. To tell anyone who will listen what I've learned about the importance of the lenses we choose and how they can change everything. In times of deepest pain and grief, and in the routine, everyday moments, and in times of great joy and celebration, we can look through a lens of faith, gratitude, and hope to discover God's presence, his provision, and his protection all around us—through the light of his love—which results in the kind of joy and peace that "exceeds anything we can understand." Don't get me wrong. There is mourning involved—grief and loss require it—but joy and peace *can* mingle in with the mourning, and eventually overtake it.

I received my cancer diagnosis on January 4, 2018, and that was the day God began to transform everything. If we could rewind, to take a peek at what my life looked like before that moment, you'd see a woman living faithfully, or at least, with *actions* that reflected my limited understanding of faithfulness.

I did my quiet time and prayer time, reading God's word and worshipping regularly. I successfully completed my performance-based checklist of "faith actions" every day. I *looked* like someone who relied on God and trusted his plan for my life, but truly I was just *talking* to God about my own plans, my worries and my fears, without ever fully releasing them. Like a toddler who's not quite ready to put away her favorite toy, I'd flash those plans and worries and fears in his general direction, smiling furtively, a little bit unsure of myself, but then I'd pull them right back to clutch close to my chest: "Here, God, I trust you to take this, but not really. I think I'll just keep it." I even remember wondering, deep down, if it was actually *possible* to release it all to him? On a logistic level? I had the daily details of our bakery business to operate, a close family with many relationships to keep, and even just the little pieces of daily life on my plate seemed too many, too reliant on me, to ever completely let go.

There's not much like the prospect of death to teach you how silly and futile it is to do anything *but* let go. When all you've got is God, you discover he's all you need.

I'm not going to say the transformation happened overnight by any stretch of the imagination. But that day, when I picked up the phone and was told I had an aggressive, invasive form of breast cancer, I began a journey into a deeper faith and a new perspective that allowed me to see God's provision and preparation in every moment that followed. It taught me to look for him everywhere, to trust in his presence, and to give him control of everything. I was able to take that lens with me, watching it continue to deepen and grow, even through the losses of my mother and daughter. As it turns out, that kind of awareness (and the peace it provides) is what makes surrender *possible*. Awareness begins with the lens you choose—with God's help and guidance.

How do we find the correct lens so that we can always see the truth of his presence? Through all the days of my life—surviving cancer, the griefs my family experienced, the ordinary days of marriage and motherhood, and the celebrations (big and small)—I have learned I can always choose a perspective that allows me to see God's light and presence. Learning this has changed me forever, and my desire in sharing this story is that *you* can experience the same life-changing lens, an outlook that proves that faith is warranted, gratitude is powerful, and hope is eternal, because God *never* forsakes us. His love endures forever, and he never changes.

God is always there, weaving things together for good, providing for us, and supporting us in every way. Like the gossamer threads of a spider's web, nearly invisible unless they catch the light, we just need to learn to truly *see* in order to catch a glimpse of his work. You know how, sometimes, wearing sunglasses allows you to see iridescence dancing over certain windows and surfaces, a glimmer and glow of color that isn't there when you look with the naked eye?

It's like that. What you see around you has everything to do with the lens you choose.

In the pages that follow, we are going to explore some of the life-giving lenses God has taught me to use, and which I hope to pass on to you. We'll explore these lenses by looking, in turn, at how we experience and approach:

- Periods of grief
- The "every days"
- Moments of celebration

In each phase of life, I truly believe that we have the opportunity to choose our lens: a lens of either fear, despair, and control; or faith, hope, and love. I pray this story will encourage you to look at your own life, the boring bits, the hard bits, and the wonderful bits alike, and discover God's presence and provision in the midst of it all. I pray you'll find the opportunities for gratitude and gain a sense of your calling to share the love and light that you have received. I pray you'll see the moments of dancing iridescence.

Let's look for good together.

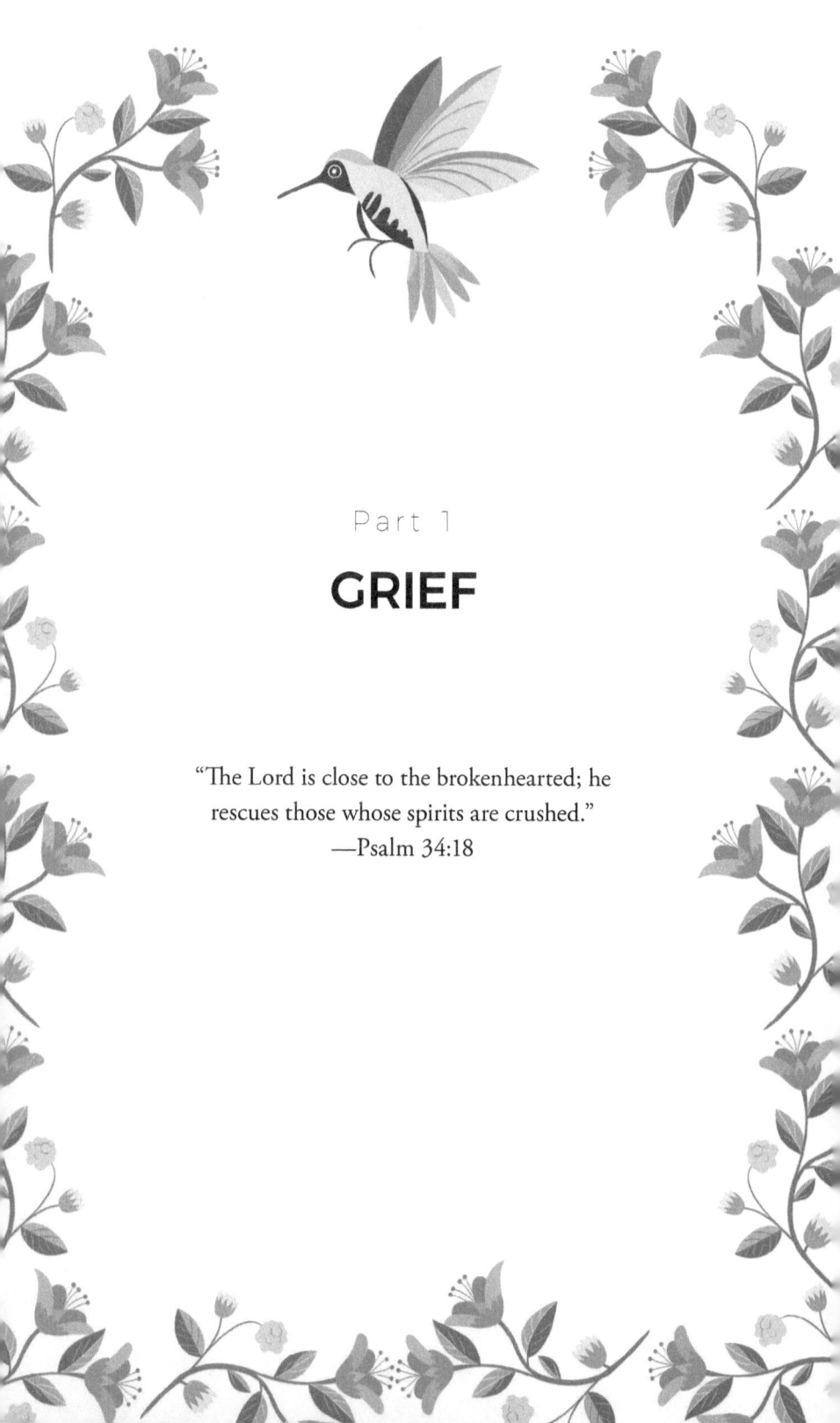

Part 1

GRIEF

"The Lord is close to the brokenhearted; he
rescues those whose spirits are crushed."
—Psalm 34:18

Chapter 1

TUNNEL VISION

T HERE ARE MOMENTS when it feels like the whole earth shifts beneath your feet (and knocks you on your butt for good measure). You look around you, and nothing is familiar—or maybe it is, a little bit, but it's all been turned on its head, or you seem to be looking at it through the light-distorting murk of deep, dark waters. Grief does funny things to how you see the world.

In moments of shock, especially, we humans tend to fall into tunnel vision. We zoom in, focusing on the object of our pain, change, or sorrow, and as our image of that object clarifies and sharpens, everything else fades away—the petty annoyances, the daily to-dos, even some of the things we thought mattered most. The world narrows down until it is filled by *nothing* but the crisis itself.

In some ways, that clarity and sharpened focus are gifts from God. In other ways, they're dangerous because you can get frozen into a permanent state of tunnel vision. The only way to move forward is to lean hard into God for guidance.

My Tunnel Vision: A Diagnosis

My own shock-induced tunnel vision began over the phone.

I had a breast cancer biopsy during the holidays—on my birthday, in fact. Then, *because* it was the holidays, I had to wait for what felt like centuries for my results. It wasn't that long, in reality. I got the phone call from the radiologist in early January.

"Well," he said, "we did find cancer, and it's not the good kind." After that, the only words I really heard were "invasive" and "aggressive." (It was, in fact, triple-negative breast cancer, or TNBC. TNBC is usually more aggressive, harder to treat, and more likely to come back than cancers that are hormone receptor-positive or HER2-positive. Triple-negative breast cancer represents 10 to 15 percent of breast cancers overall.)

While waiting on the biopsy results, I had been in what I call optimistic denial. I think I actually stayed there for quite some time following the diagnosis too. I didn't embrace reality, at least not at first. Instead, I hyper-focused on unexpected things. I'm a pretty "crunchy" person, so I started by arguing with God (and the doctors) about chemo. I was sure we could combat the disease without poisoning my whole body, that there were alternatives, and that I wouldn't have to lose my hair. Goodness, I did *not* want to lose my hair. That was a real obsession for quite a while.

Tunnel vision can be so helpful, but only if it's paired with clarity of mind, trust in God, and some level of willingness to *take action*. Thank Jesus, I had a clear-eyed husband and a logical, empathetic medical team who quickly convinced me that we needed to treat the cancer immediately and with whatever tools God had made available. I remember Bryan saying, "Honey, I don't think this is something we should spend all our time researching. God has put these people in your life for a reason, and we just need to follow." His discernment widened my myopic lens just enough to make a little more room for faith and for action to gain peace in the doctor's guidance.

The Mixed Blessing of Tunnel Vision

I stayed in pseudo-denial for a while, but I followed the steps laid out to me as the pleas of "We have to treat this ASAP!" continued to echo. As we moved forward into treatment, my tunnel vision stuck around. It's what allowed us all to do what needed to be done—that narrow focus got things moving *so* quickly and efficiently, just as it was meant to do.

It felt sometimes, with the incredibly time-consuming nature of my treatment plan, that I could barely see more than an inch from my nose: everything had become about me, my needs, my sickness, my healing. If you've been through cancer treatment, or walked beside someone going through it, then you know—it's a weird thing. Medicine is just weird. First, there's baseline medical testing, and the placement of a port in your body, a strange and uncomfortable experience on its own. Then there's the cold flow of toxic healing, and the painful injections you need in order to regrow all the white blood cells that are getting knocked out by "friendly fire."

You're sitting there for hours on steroids and Benadryl, watching whatever television programming is in front of you, with this horrible red liquid trickling through you. (It is nicknamed the "red devil" treatment, though I had a friend who balked at the idea of giving Satan any credit for my healing. She christened it "God juice" instead.) You're miserably uncomfortable. Everyone around you is asking what they can do to help. Your "real life" grinds to a halt.

I'll tell you what, the way your whole life narrows down like that is such a mixed blessing. On the one hand, it protects you from the naysayers and busybodies who want to know the details of your situation, to advise you on what you ought to be doing. That's something I learned quickly: everyone seems to have an opinion when it comes to cancer treatment, and everyone wants to grill you about it, primarily out of a place of their fear and desire to control their own situation. Luckily, you're too "in the zone" (a.k.a. exhausted and self-focused) to pay any heed to what they think, and that truly is a wonderful thing. It saves you additional doubt and grief. And there's the added bonus that, when you have an all-encompassing *thing* going on in your life, you're given leave by society at large to brush off a lot of the petty and routine details.

When I was battling cancer, my focus was squarely on myself: on my changing body, on getting better. That was all my life was about, for that time. So, if I couldn't keep a previous business or volunteer commitment? "Well, of course you can't." Too tired to think? Catching a nap at three in the afternoon? Need someone else to handle dinners for a while? Need to shirk your everyday responsibilities (because of course you do, you're in the midst of treatment, not just sitting around twiddling your thumbs)? If you have a good community, they've got you. And praise God for that. That's how it should be: your tunnel vision is *necessary*, and those in the midst of something traumatic should be supported and enabled to keep that narrow, heightened lens. You, too, should be allowed to focus *only* on what matters in those moments of grief, change, and challenge, just like I was empowered to do.

On the other hand, like I've mentioned before, tunnel vision can result in paralysis, plain and simple. My daughter, Elayna, strongly suspected something was wrong when she discovered a suspicious spot on her chest, and she zoomed straight into that paralyzing kind of tunnel vision: the tunnel vision of fear. Instead of springing into action, she allowed her fear to erase reason, practicality, and logic; she just froze. She put off getting her own biopsy, which delayed her treatment and contributed to the tragedy that followed.

(Each of the cancers that our family experienced was different, and it is not prudent to try to compare. So I am not saying that earlier action on Elayna's part would have guaranteed survival, but the fear-fueled delays did not serve her well mentally, emotionally, or physically.)

Elayna's tunnel vision prevented action at first. When she did finally go to see a doctor, the ironic thing? It was like a switch had been flipped. The truth set her free from her fear. She was finally at peace with her journey, knowing Jesus would be with her through it and for eternity.

Because, again, that's the thing about tunnel vision. If it's not joined by faith and action, it'll freeze you in place. It *can* be a blessing, as long as you lean on God to guide you and take trusting steps forward.

It's Not Just Me

Of course, tunnel vision isn't something experienced only by people in the midst of cancer treatment, like me. Tunnel vision tends to take over in many other corners of life too, and like in my situation and Elayna's, sometimes it's helpful, and sometimes it's harmful.

Parents know this well. Think about it. When you're worrying yourself silly about your kids—their decisions, their future, the risks you can see but they can't—it's easy to get so locked in on them that you forget to live your own life. At some point, you have to release what you do not control. You can pray. You can give advice when asked. But you *cannot* force an outcome. It's hard to see that from within your myopic worry.

Tunnel vision also likes to show up whenever life blindsides you: a business failure, a false accusation, a natural disaster. These experiences demand your full attention, and they should. But they can also freeze you in place if you never take a small step back. Obsessing over something is not the same as action. There has to be a turning point where you widen your vision and begin to move forward again.

And in grief and in loss, especially, the world shrinks down to one piercing reality: the person who is gone, the future that's been lost. In those moments, you *may* find yourself unnervingly present, crystal clear and acutely aware of every detail, or else floating above yourself, unable to process what's happening. Both are protective mechanisms. If you had to carry the whole weight at once, you would be crushed.

If you stay in tunnel vision too long, fear and stress will have an impact on your body. You need ways to widen the lens again, to remember that life is larger than the crisis in front of you. Gratitude is one way, and that's an attitude you can take with you into all corners of life. Naming the good and beautiful gifts all around you can help you stretch past the tunnel. Gratitude doesn't erase the loss or the struggle, but it expands your vision just enough to keep going. More on that later.

Tunnel vision can be a strange mercy, stripping life down to what matters most. But it can also trap us in fear or paralysis. The key is knowing when to zoom in, when to zoom out, and always, always letting God adjust the lens.

CHAPTER 2

COMPASSION AND PATIENCE: LET THE LITTLE THINGS STAY LITTLE

TUNNEL VISION REDUCES life down to the essentials. The petty things fade. That kind of focus can be clarifying and, dare I say, even holy? But the intensity of grief, or a life-and-death situation, accomplishes something *more* than just that urgent, focused "zooming in"—there's also a broader unfolding happening in the background, a deepening of empathy and gratitude.

Your line of sight shifts, reminding you of what really matters. Everything regains its proper proportion, with the little things staying little instead of distorting, funhouse mirror-style, into massive, frustrating distractions. You gain a new, gentler, more patient lens, particularly in regard to how you view and treat others.

Seeing Others Differently

I remember once, when I was in the depths of treatment, being bored silly by the conversation taking place around me. Whoever I was with was having the most trivial, gossipy discussion about what someone else had worn to church, and I couldn't help thinking, "I just truly could not care less right now." It seemed like such a petty thing to even think about, let alone discuss out loud with others—someone else's clothing choices, really?—*especially* when I was busy fighting a battle for my very life. At the same time, I worked to quell my rising irritation at the speakers around me. Being bothered by their gossip, too, did not seem *worth it* in that moment.

In fact, I'd say that it's easier in general to forgive or excuse other people's little mistakes and selfish moments during times of deep suffering, change, or grief, because you yourself are experiencing a massive shift in focus and priorities. With so much already on your own plate, it's just less stressful to learn to let those little things go. Surrender can be a liberating action that filters out unnecessary thoughts of judgment.

Some angry guy cuts you off in traffic? Instead of muttering curses in his general direction, you may find yourself wondering if he's OK. What could be happening in his life to make him speed ahead like that when everyone else is kindly "zippering" back and forth to let each other into the only open lane? Maybe a loved one just received a sobering diagnosis, or he's rushing off to the hospital with his wife in labor next to him. Who knows? That's the point.

As another example, maybe the cashier is distracted and inattentive while you wait in the checkout line. Instead of impatiently tapping your toe, you'll find yourself extending grace, wondering if she was up all night with a colicky baby, or maybe her mom is sick, or maybe she's going through a horrible breakup, or . . . or . . . or . . .

My point is *we don't know what others are going through.* What harm is there in assuming the best of others, instead of the worst? Especially when their petty offenses against us are the tiniest, most insignificant of things in light of the hugeness of life and death and love and God? Why would we not offer those around us *more* grace, rather than less, especially during our *own* hardest times? What point is there in allowing ourselves to get offended by the perceived slights of those around us, or the little inconveniences we experience at the hands of strangers, when we don't even know their story and have exactly zero right to judge? Especially as we struggle through our own darkest valleys, and (most likely) have moments of thoughtlessness or selfish irritability ourselves?

I continued showing up to work at the bakery during my chemo treatments, and I remember a young man whose eyes lingered on my bald head hidden under its cute cap, my puffy face devoid of brows or lashes. He recognized the look and quietly said, "From the looks of things, I think you may be going through the same tough time as my grandma. If that's true, God bless you."

I almost cried at his compassionate, unintrusive words. May we all have that young man's attentive, discerning eye.

My mother brought a similar lens to her whole life. Her deep compassion was obvious in the prayers she sent out via text to anyone around her when they went through hard times: job searches, grown children making unwise choices, their own physical trials—whatever the situation, my mom was the rock for her friends who lifted every request to God.

My daughter Elayna, too, was generous in giving and modeling grace to others during her own cancer journey. Even though she knew her time on earth was limited, she would not allow those around her to cling to fear for themselves, because she knew the danger of letting that paralyzing agent control your life.

When the realities of life and death became part of my daily thoughts throughout my chemo treatments, the trivial parts of life became simply silly. When a tragedy strikes, we often also receive a new kind of empathy that allows us to see beyond the surface, past negative actions, to the sublayer of pain, fear, and sadness. It's like a superpower: X-ray vision. Personally, I found my heart was softer during that time, and that I made fewer snap judgments. I could more easily see the humanity within others and follow Jesus's command: "Love each other. Just as I have loved you, you should love each other. Your love for one another will prove to the world that you are my disciples."

We never know what others are going through. Grief and suffering allow us to remember that fact, refocus our lenses, and extend compassion.

Compassion Is a Choice

I don't want to make it sound like anyone who is in the depths of suffering is automatically and effortlessly transported to saintlike levels of compassion and patient, forgiving empathy. Sometimes the opposite is true.

Fear, physical pain, and grief manifest differently in different people—and may show up differently at different times in the *same* people. It's easy to fall into the trap of self-centered suffering, becoming grumpy about every little thing and demanding, "I'm sick, so do what I want or get out of my way." I call it playing the "cancer card," using my hardship to gain some sympathetic clout. That's where you wind up if you allow the tunnel vision to narrow a bit too far and a bit too stubbornly, warping into entitlement. Instead of learning to recognize that *everyone is going through something*, you can't see beyond what *you* are going through, and you demand that everyone around you focus solely on you too. Misery loves preferential treatment.

Cancer wards aren't just full of happy, compassionate sick people. A lot of them are downright angry, and of course, that's understandable. I didn't just wake up the day after my diagnosis and feel a sudden God-given love for the world. That compassion was something I learned over time, and often through embarrassingly revealing moments.

Let's return to the angry driver cutting to the front of the line, rather than politely merging. Say that, after watching him do that, I think something like, "Oh my gosh, God, did you see what that jerk just did?" Then about ten minutes later, after spacing out a bit and nearly missing my exit, I do the exact same thing to someone else. Whoops. A lot of my learning looked something like that: any time I started to feel a bit prideful or entitled, thinking I was justified in leaning on my illness as an excuse for my own mistakes or selfish little choices, God would turn the lens to selfie mode, giving me an unflattering angle of myself. Like a parent gently pointing out a child's selfishness, God would say, "My child, you're reacting from a place of pain. Can you see the hypocrisy in using your situation as an excuse? Extend my grace to others. Instead of acting with irritation or blame, ask yourself what *they* might be going through. This is my loving way. This is how I see each of my children."

I started there. Slowly, I found my compassion and patience deepening and growing as God's loving and gracious lens took over.

Patience and Appreciation for the Little Things

It always makes me laugh when the guy bagging my groceries answers my question of "How are you?" with "I woke up this morning, so I am blessed to be alive." That's all we can really ask for, isn't it? It's a simplistic appreciation of the gift of life—the goodness of the fact of our continuing existence, in spite of whatever little inconveniences the world may throw our way—but it's kind of true. Praise God, we're alive. When the improbable beauty of that reality really sinks in, or when it's no longer taken for granted, the petty things melt away, and I'm no longer just talking about other people's mistakes or unkindnesses. God gives us *more* than compassion, if we choose to accept it, during our darkest and most difficult times; he also gives us supernatural patience. All the little things get put in their proper place. *The little stays little.*

You catch your sleeve on the door handle, something that usually fills you with illogical levels of rage. But instead of grumping and growling as always, you catch yourself thinking: "Hey, at least I managed to get out of bed today. I'm up and walking around." And then you wonder why something so little ever bothered you in the first place, before your treatment, or your loss, or whatever it may be. You have a new lens, and the world around you becomes a bit like an impressionist painting as all the imperfections blur together and fade into the overarching, beautiful *good*.

Because it *is* so good to be alive. Who do I think I am to expect my life to be so perfectly perfect, with no bumps at all, that I could write it all out in pen without ever needing an eraser? Life is *meant* to have texture and friction. How boring would life be, visually speaking, if it were all easy and perfectly smooth? With no contrast, no depth, all smooth surfaces? Life isn't life if stuff doesn't happen, and that includes the little inconveniences.

I recently got quite sick and spent two days in bed. Lying there like that triggered so many memories of my chemo, and the absolute mind-numbing uneventfulness of just lying in bed for days, hoping and wishing that I could feel better again. Wishing I could stand up, even if that meant I might stub my toe. Wishing I could cook myself a meal, even if that meant I had to deal with the dishes afterward.

A loss, a life-and-death experience, a trauma, one of the hidden blessings that comes along with that kind of pain is a lens that sets the little things back in their place, keeping them little, and even allowing you to appreciate them.

Pass It On

Tunnel vision helped me focus on what was urgent during my cancer treatment. But stepping back a bit broadened my view again in a way that reminded me of what was important, and what really wasn't. That guy cutting me off in traffic—what's more important, his soul and well-being, or my irritation? I found myself continually asking how I can learn to see others, even *that guy*, through God's eyes.

And this is something you can teach your children to do too: tell them, "You don't know what the bully is going through." Maybe the bully doesn't know how to express emotions any other way. As parents, we set the example. We can ask questions and have conversations to learn, then teach our little ones how to spread grace and mercy and compassion.

Life isn't meant to be smooth—it's meant to be textured. And the rough edges are often what teach us how to love. This is something I've always hoped to teach my own children, urging them to ask themselves what others might be going through, and if their little offenses are worth getting worked up over in light of eternity. In that way, I hope I've been a part of God's effort to spread grace and mercy, patience and compassion. Life is not fair, but we can learn to let God dole out justice and pray for his lens of grace and mercy—even when we are deep in an emotional injustice.

Speaking of our children. My darkest moment had a staggering impact on the lens I brought to what it meant to care for others, my children included, during the darkest valleys. Let's talk about empathy, control, and surrender next.

Chapter 3

YOU CAN'T CONTROL THE PANORAMA

AVE YOU EVER tried to take a panoramic photo? All you have to do is hold your phone steady and slowly, slowly sweep it from one side to the other in order to capture a full picture. It's easy enough if you're dealing with a stationary scene, but not so simple when there are people involved. If anyone moves even a muscle, weird distortions show up in the final image, and the whole thing appears unreal (and definitely unframeable).

That's the problem with panoramas. They only work if every single component falls into line, and guess what? They probably won't, at least not the way you want or expect, because *you* don't reign over the room.

When I was going through cancer treatment, as well as in the grieving periods following my mom's death and then Elayna's, I tried so hard to keep everyone and everything around me under my control—though I never would have admitted that was what I was after. I felt responsible for the well-being and emotions of my loved ones, especially my children. I acted as if it was all on *me* to hold the camera nice and still, making sure everything was in place and everyone was OK, hoping the big picture would develop into my own personal version of "just right." God was quick to teach me, though, that I could not control the panorama, not even one little bit. And what a relief that turned out to be.

Empathy Versus Control

When you love people deeply, empathy comes naturally, and that's a blessing from God. But it's so easy for that empathy to morph into a compulsion to control.

In the months of grief I experienced throughout my own cancer and the losses of Elayna and my mother, I started every day by going through a mental checklist: "How's Kailey? How's Russell? How's Nate? How are the kids? Is Bryan OK? Is everyone dealing with their feelings well right now? Is it a good day?" As if any of those questions had answers that were remotely within my control. As if those questions represented the catalog of my personal daily duties.

It was hard, above all else, to release my feelings of responsibility when it came to my children.

Our son, Nate, was only a few years out of college and working a high-stress job when his sister died. As an engineer, he was responsible for details on large projects, but the grief clouded his thoughts. Most twenty-something year olds don't experience such traumatic loss; there really isn't a road map or experienced friends to walk you through it. Watching him navigate his demanding career through these new emotions, experiencing waves of grief and missing his sister, was so hard. I wanted to fix it—I wanted to fix everybody.

My young grandchildren, whether it was their mom or their aunt, each one had lost someone they cared deeply for, and oh, how I wanted to help them through it. I felt such a need to control each family member and family unit. I thought that if everyone was OK at the same time on the same day, then I could be OK. But this was just a distracting subconscious lie I was living, an attempt to control the uncontrollables: other people, and the complexities of grief.

I was avoiding my own emotions by attempting to tend to others. It's far easier to take action outward rather than ponder inward when grief is involved, at least for me. I hated the natural, negative emotions that threatened to flood and overwhelm my own heart, and I worried about my loved ones who were feeling that same yuckiness—so I tried to fight it off for all of us, the heroic defender of the whole family. I didn't realize this was the case, that I was trying to control the panorama, until we got the opportunity to take a twenty-day road trip in the summer after Elayna died. We'll return to that story a little later.

During this time, I recall saying regularly how much I hate negative emotions—sadness, despair, longing—but also immediately realizing, "Well, of course. Who doesn't?" Of *course*, we don't like them; they feel bad, and we live in a world where the question, "What's your pain level?" (accompanied by a gesture toward a chart of smiley faces in various stages of contentment and discomfort) is often closely followed by a sensation-dulling prescription. We all want to live in happy-face land. Success is equated with zero pain.

Yet pain has purpose. We have just been trained to focus on pleasure more than on reality. This focus has come at the detriment of learning and teaching healthy coping mechanisms to the next generation. Emotional pain must be felt and experienced. We *can* learn how to pause during pain in order to process and grow through it. As we learn and survive, we can teach others the benefits of living through the ebbs and flows of a healthy emotional life.

In the end, all my worry over other people's emotional experiences took a physical toll. Silly, silly me. My body called me out on my futile battle against emotion, as all those misplaced feelings of responsibility made me literally sick with anxiety—me, the least "anxious" one in the family.

Being *There* Versus Being Responsible

God began to show me the crucial difference: teaching me that I can be *there* for people without being *responsible* for them.

For example, I think of all the worries I held in my heart about my sister during those difficult months. She and Mom were so close. They were best friends and confidants, and she was deeply connected to Elayna as well. While I'm the comedian of the family, she's the philosopher, the brilliant one, and a nurse to boot—so she had a better understanding than the rest of us when it came to the seriousness of the illnesses blasting through our family. I worried so much about her grieving process, a process that wasn't my responsibility to manage in the slightest.

Being present, listening, shedding tears together? Absolutely, that's what God asked of me during that time. Responsibility for my sister's heart, the hearts of my children, though—that responsibility belonged solely to God.

God Has No Grandchildren

And who better to trust with that great, big task than the Father of us all?

My obsessive, controlling empathy began to ebb away during prayer time one day, when I clearly heard God remind me: "Your loved ones' feelings are not your responsibility. I've got them. *I have no grandchildren.* I know and desire the best for all of my children."

God has no grandchildren. He is Father to us all.

I finally learned the depth of what that statement means during the road trip my husband, Bryan, and I took the summer after Elayna's death.

Bryan and I enjoy planning trips and looking forward to the time away from routines and details. We enjoy being together, so we decided a road trip would be a perfect opportunity for release and resetting. We drove west through Arizona, Nevada, Utah, and Colorado, hiking in national parks and enjoying the drive and time together in the car. It was cathartic—quiet time in nature in prayer.

This was when I finally, slowly realized that I cannot control others, nor am I responsible for them. God loves each of us. He wants each of us to surrender our pain, hurt, and sadness to him. During our trip, I finally saw that I was still me—there was light and hope again. My grief was no longer crippling me physically. I gradually began to produce endorphins through exercise. I felt a peace and hope that I hadn't remembered completely for months.

God works everything together for good. He knows, better than we ever could, when someone may need to laugh, or be comforted, or simply feel the pain. It's a tapestry that only the Creator himself could manage, nurturing every person however they need to be nurtured. Everyone's grief and experience is different, and only God truly *gets it*.

It took a while, but I came to understand and accept that God doesn't love my children, my sister, or my family through me. He has a direct, intimate relationship with each of them. He alone knows what they need. *That's* what he meant when he told me he had no grandchildren.

All I have is my narrow "Kathy lens," and there was never a chance I could manage everyone's feelings for them from that perspective. *He* has the only true, all-encompassing view.

Let It Go, Let It Go

Realizing that Father God alone is responsible for each and every person's heart allowed me to (slowly and imperfectly) let go. I grew more and more able to release my self-imposed checklist, my illusion of control, my need to manage how other people experience their grief. When we returned from our road trip, I was able to allow each family member to feel, as the feelings came without stress or panic that normalcy would never return.

Again: every grief is different. There's no handbook or template. My loved ones had to feel their own feelings, and so did I, because unfelt feelings don't simply disappear. They just burrow deeper to fester and wait. And you can't feel someone else's feelings for them.

Letting go doesn't mean not caring—of course not. It just means trusting God to love on the people I love better than I ever could, more than I ever could. It means trusting him to work it all together and provide in ways I could never predict or orchestrate. Prayer, instead of grasping for control, has become my outlet when I see my loved ones struggling.

Releasing the panorama to God means putting down the camera and relinquishing my perfect vision for the photo. My job is just to accept my own lens, limited and human as it may be, and trust my loved ones' hearts and feelings to the one who sees it all.

Chapter 4

EMOTIONS: LIVING INTO ALL LIFE'S COLORS

I N THE LAST chapter, I shared how I tried to manage other people's emotions during periods of grief, working to smooth away their pain instead of tending to my own uncomfortable feelings. That's a selfish kind of urge to have, really—and in part, I was doing it to distract myself from the messy, unpredictable business of my own suffering. At times, it also came from my desire not to be inconvenienced by *their* feelings. I wanted everyone else to be fine, so that *I* could be fine. I wanted all the ducks to be in a row, and I wanted them all to be happy little ducks.

Dumb, isn't it? I'm not going to say it's exclusively a "mom thing," but I think that urge—to shout, "*You* better have a good day, because *I* want to have a good day!"—is one that will feel familiar to a lot of parents. We just want our kids to be happy, we trick ourselves into thinking it's our *job* to make them happy, and it can be hard to shake off the tendency to let our morale sink or float based on how well we think we're doing on that goal. Too many of us live the mantra,

"I am only as happy as my saddest child." This should not be true, nor should the pressure be put upon our kids to "make us happy" by being happy or OK themselves.

I'm saying this to you, but I'm saying it to me too: emotions are beneficial and necessary. All of them, not just the obviously positive ones. The good, the bad, and the ugly, we were made to feel them all, and we don't have to let others' feelings dictate ours. If someone's having a hard time, why the heck wouldn't I try to be the bright spot in their day instead of letting myself be dragged down to join them? Why would I try to prevent my loved ones from working through their personal hardships when I know how much I've grown and learned from my own? Why can't I, as those in the Jewish tradition do, sit shiva with my loved ones in their mourning, showing up with quiet kindness and Jesus's own compassion, letting them feel their feels instead of trying to fix things for them? And can't I extend that same kind of acceptance and grace to myself?

Today, I can testify to how important it is to feel all the feels, *especially* during dark times. But back then, I fought off my own negative emotions, as well as others', with all my might and in a myriad of ways.

In the months that followed the compounded grief of losing both Mom and Elayna, I cycled through just about every avoidance tactic you can imagine. Focusing on and managing others' emotional experiences? Check. Binge-watching happy movies and my favorite shows? Check. Eating my way through my comfort foods? Check. Enjoying a fun tequila cocktail by the pool? Check. When the endorphins didn't come from my regular exercise, I tried to relax them away instead, even though what I called "relaxing" ultimately wasn't even enjoyable, in the end. I got no real pleasure out of my tequila drink. I was trying to get my body to chill out, to stop feeling, to go numb, but I was just creating anxiety for myself instead.

Numbness doesn't work because it doesn't make the pain go away. It pushes it down for a while, sure, but then it just sits there, and the pressure builds. Eventually, like the pressure cooker in the kitchen, that steam will find a way to get out—either by exploding or through an intentional, methodical release.

Acceptance Versus Numbness

I broke out of my own carefully cultivated numbness thanks to an unintentional little blessing: a flash of anger. I got mad that my "relaxing" wasn't working. Specifically, I was upset that my tequila cocktail wasn't giving me the least bit of joy or calm anymore. In a fit of angry determination, I told myself I'd just quit drinking alcohol completely for one year and see what happened. So I did.

The clarity that came after I made that choice was unexpected. I remember thinking, *Aw man, I didn't even realize I was avoiding all these feelings, but now I'm going to have to feel them.* And I did feel them. I accepted my grief, faced the anger and ache head-on, and that created progress. Then the next time around, it wasn't quite as hard. I learned from feeling both the negative and the positive—a huge step. Thank you, God.

The work of processing grief looks different for everyone, but it's always *hard* work. Necessary work, if we want to be well. Part of the task is figuring out what that looks like for you. What helps you process? Deep breathing, journaling, a walk in the sunshine, an hour of prayer, coffee with a friend? What do you need to do in order to let yourself feel all the feels? Figure it out, however you can. The result will be worth it, and you'll be able to empathize and encourage others in new ways. If *I* were (eventually) able to do it—anxiety-avoidant and stubborn as I am—then I know that you can too.

Grief is a bell and a ball in a box. At first, every time the box jostles the slightest bit, the ball rings the bell. Every little thing is a reminder that resounds through you and shakes you up.

As you work through your situation and feelings, accepting and processing your emotions in healthy ways, the ball continues to rattle around, but the bell—your pain—has gotten smaller and smaller. The ringing isn't as constant or as overwhelming. The grief hasn't gone away, but it's subsided. You can breathe freely and deeply again.

Feel the Rainbow

We wouldn't really know what happiness is without the contrast of sadness.

Life is meant to contain all the textures and shades—all the emotions. We need *all* of it, the full range of color, that depth of perspective. Otherwise, we're choosing to live in a grayscale world, instead of embracing the full, beautiful rainbow.

Grief, when processed well, teaches you to truly feel the wide range of feelings that come bubbling to the surface. For me, that learning happened on a personal, individual level—and we had to learn it together, as a family, as well.

When a family gathers together shortly after a loss, you feel the gap in your ranks so acutely. You spend your time together, missing the person who's gone. You feel the wrongness of an absent note, a layer that's been removed from the composite that is your family, so everything feels somehow thin and shallow and incomplete.

Then, as time passes, the loved one's essence starts showing up in those gatherings again, through the sharing of favorite memories and funny stories, or little comments like "Oh, this would have driven her nuts." You find a new depth again through that remembering, and you start seeing that the absent person is still impacting you all. Her fingerprints are still there, pressed into the very fibers of your conversations and togetherness. There's a familiar light being cast over you all, the light you remember emanating from their personality and nature when they were still with you. As a family, you've accepted their physical absence, and you've found peace in their memory.

That was a huge piece of my personal grieving process too: being able to cherish the good things that *did* occur, instead of only lamenting the lost future. It breaks my heart that Elayna died at twenty-nine, and I never got to see her in her thirties or beyond. At the same time, hey, she never had to experience the discomforts of age. In those quick five months between her diagnosis and when she became too sick to do much of anything, we squeezed in a lifetime of moments. We threw a viewing party for a partial eclipse, had a joy-packed Christmas where all the big-personality members of the family got along for three days under the same roof, and absolutely maximized the memory-making in ways we wouldn't have otherwise. We lived *fully* in that little window of time. I think about Elayna today, and I feel a colorful swirl of joy and grief, gratitude and love.

Same with Mom. Before she died, we threw her a huge eightieth birthday celebration—her last earth-side birthday. She was at her happy place (the beach) with all the people she loved (her girls, her grandkids, her great-grandkids). We ate birthday cake and fried shrimp, did jigsaw puzzles, and just spent time together, making incredible memories. Those memories remain as happy hues that now provide balance against the darker shades of missing her.

Letting myself feel my negative emotions didn't erase the pain, but it allowed me to process, and it gave me contrast. You can't appreciate the brilliance of the silver moon in the daylight without the deep, velvety blue-black of the nighttime sky.

Uncomfortable Kindness

A quick sidenote about one other risk of allowing ourselves to avoid uncomfortable emotions, in ourselves and in others. I mentioned earlier the Jewish practice of sitting shiva: accompanying others through their grief by simply, lovingly showing up. If we don't learn to get comfortable with the full range of emotions during our own moments of pain and grief, we won't be able to be there when those we love are in the depths, either.

When I learned that a friend's daughter had survived the tragedy of the floods that ripped through summer camps in Texas, I wanted to write her a card, but I tore up three whole drafts before I finally sent one. I was just terrified I'd say the wrong thing.

Looking back, I can see that I almost let my own fear and discomfort rob me of the chance to simply say, "I don't know what to say, but I care. I love you. I'm praying for you."

People care that you care, and it's never the wrong time to be kind. The Bible says it over and over again: *love one another*. Sometimes that means showing up, even if you don't know the right words to say. I termed it uncomfortable kindness, doing the right and kind thing even though it makes you uncomfortable to take that risk, because you know that loving in full color is worth it.

What Our Emotions Teach Us

Every emotion we feel is an opportunity to learn, grow, and be enhanced in who we are. If my experiences with grief and loss have taught me anything, it's to always ask God: "What do you want me to *learn* from this?"

Maybe the lesson will be: emotions aren't trustworthy, but I can depend on God and his true word to reveal the truth.

Maybe the lesson will be: we *all* go through pain, and now I can understand others in ways I couldn't before, extending compassion more easily even to people who differ from me or whose actions I don't fully comprehend.

Maybe the lesson will be: everyone experiences life differently, and for some, the losses are greater than we might think. I lost a mother and a daughter; that doesn't make someone else's loss of a pet, a job, a marriage, or their mobility a lesser thing, not in the slightest. We can have grace and empathy for *everyone*, and it will be easier if we acknowledge and work through our own feelings first.

You can gain a depth of appreciation for humanity when you experience loss, a richness of caring and perspective—but only if you remember to ask God, "What do you want me to learn from this, so that I can be better at loving other people?" The Bible reminds us what a wonderful God we have—he is the Father of our Lord Jesus Christ, the source of every mercy, and the one who so wonderfully comforts and strengthens us in our hardships and trials. And why does he do this? So that when others are troubled, needing our sympathy and encouragement, we can pass on to them this same help and comfort God has given us.

And of course, that's not to say those who have never experienced deep loss can't be empathetic and compassionate too, not at all. Learning from the daily disappointments, the lesser griefs, is a choice as well. Strength builds in all types of resistance and hard times. We grow beyond the complacency that leaves us in a comfortable stagnation.

The takeaway is this: no matter how "big" or "small" we think the hardships we face are, always make a point to ask God to teach you through them. Feel the feelings, and let God help you grow.

Living Without Regret

We all learn different things from our hardest times, but here's where all my grief and personal processing led me: it's given me peace. I don't have regrets. I was a good daughter. I was a good mom. I can rest easy in the knowledge that the people I lost *knew* they were loved, and that makes it good. That truth steadies me on the days when grief still rings the bell.

And if I could speak directly to you, I'd want you to know this: you are loved too. God loves you with a perfect, unending love. If I knew you personally, I'm sure I'd love you too.

Don't let emotional wounds, unaddressed and still festering, keep you in a black and white world that keeps you *safe* from bumping the dirty wound of past trauma, grief, or loss. Let healed emotion color your life. The whole spectrum—the light and the dark, the vibrant and the muted. Feel it, learn from it, let it shape you. In the end, it's not only about your own healing. It's about becoming the kind of person who can hold out love and empathy to others, in full and living color.

Chapter 5

SEEK OUT THE GLIMMERS

GRIEF TRANSFORMED MY lens on life. My own cancer journey, and the losses of my daughter and mother, brought me into and through the intense, mixed blessing of tunnel vision. Those experiences also taught me to do a better job of viewing the world and others with patience and compassion, to release my loved ones to God, and to embrace the full spectrum of human emotions.

Above all else, my times of grief have given me a lens to see God's faithfulness at work all around me. Grief has taught me to seek out the glimmers of iridescence he makes visible to us every day, to look for and notice the shimmer of the thin, dewdrop-beaded threads he leaves behind as he weaves all things together for good.

I can't explain how completely my lens has been transformed without mentioning something that happened during all my cancer treatment's "times of waiting"—doctors, chemo, rest, recovery. While reading my Bible during those long, quiet moments, I came across some verses my aunt had shared with me years before:

When I think of all this, I fall to my knees and pray to the Father, the Creator of everything in heaven and on earth. I pray that *from his glorious, unlimited resources he will empower you with inner strength through his Spirit.* Then *Christ will make his home in your hearts as you trust in him. Your roots will grow down into God's love* and keep you strong. And may you have the power to understand, as all God's people should, *how wide, how long, how high, and how deep his love is. May you experience the love of Christ, though it is too great to understand fully.* Then you will be made complete with all the fullness of life and power that comes from God.

Now all glory to God, who is able, through his mighty power at work within us, *to accomplish infinitely more than we might ask or think.* Glory to him in the church and in Christ Jesus through all generations forever and ever! Amen.

These became my life verses, God's promise that gives me hope and focus on what is real and possible. I never would have found them without the right lens.

Wearing the Right Lens

When I started looking around for signs of God's faithfulness all around me—when my grief and forced pauses invited me to try on a new, glimmer-seeking lens—I saw his light absolutely everywhere.

Sometimes he showed up in paradox. When I was going through chemo, people could tell right away. No eyebrows, no eyelashes, a hat pulled down, it was just obvious. That visibility was no fun, but it gave me unique opportunities. Strangers asked questions. I could share my story. I could say, "God's taking care of me," and it didn't come across as preaching, because it was clearly, simply the truth. There's a silver lining for you. The opportunity to share my faith in such a loving, natural, and impactful way—that was a real glimmer.

God's provision showed up in so many other ways, once I started looking for it, and especially through the actions of other people: the manager I found for my bakery business at just the right time, who coincidentally only needed the job during the exact months I was in treatment. Two friends who sent a handwritten card every single week, faithfully; the kind of steady encouragement that carried me through. Unexpected checks in the mail, a fifty-dollar bill slipped into my hand with the words, "God told me you might need this for parking." A hug from an old friend out of the blue.

Those were all glimmers. People obeying God's nudge, looking through a compassionate lens themselves, becoming his hands and feet. Their kindness was evidence of God at work, shimmering across the surface of everything I could see.

The Ripple Effect

Here's a beautiful thing: those glimmers don't stop with the person who receives them. When someone obeys God's prompting, both giver and receiver are blessed. And when others witness that exchange, they're blessed too. It's a ripple effect of God's presence, spreading outward.

Sometimes I think, *What if those kind people who showed Christ to me during my hardest time simply hadn't?* What if they had shrugged off the thought to write a card, or send that fifty dollars, or step in to help? We'd have missed the opportunity to work together as God designed us to—to take what we've learned through hard experiences and use it to bless others. That's what makes even the hardest seasons worth it. I don't regret what I've gone through, because it's made me better equipped to love.

I think, too, of the friends my daughter Elayna left behind, and how I connected with them in new ways after her passing.

Elayna was the go-to girl in her friend group. A gifted discerner even as a young child, her insights and rebuttals to our parenting directives stood out in a wise and logical way, usually accurate and worth pondering. As a young adult, she continued sharing that gift as a good listener with empathy and relatability. To her friends, she was the *best* friend, the person you spill all to about your relationship dilemmas, exciting engagement, or pregnancy news. After Elayna's death, many of her friends, completely devastated, would reach out to let me know how much she valued my mothering—and how often she brought my perspective into her advice or guidance, saying, "Well, my mom says . . ."

One of God's glimmers, a shimmer of his spider-silk weaving in action, came from my new relationship with these caring young ladies in Elayna's absence. They still text me photo memories as they pop up, and include us in milestone celebrations and memorial events. In fact, these sweet connections were the impetus for my podcast, "Your Best Friend's Mom." A podcast was an outlet I never would have otherwise desired to pursue, in spite of encouragement from my daughters in past years. And what a special joy I have experienced from God's empowerment and provision of topics: real-world struggles around being a stronger Christ-follower.

As God gives me the word, the love, and the Bible verses to encourage and *share* his love, I envision my daughters' friends with every single script and recording. This opportunity to share truth in love would have never emerged without the loss of young Elayna.

Now *there's* a ripple for you.

Glimmers in the Mirror

There were portions of my journey through cancer and grief when it was very difficult to clear my vision in order to see God's goodness and faithfulness. One of my blurriest points had to do with my fear of losing my long, dark, thick hair, hair that I cherished and identified with so strongly—maybe even a little too much? But it's a common story that I hear from other cancer survivors, that sadness over going bald.

Throughout my aggressive chemo treatments, I begged God to let me keep my hair. Yet with each urgent prayer, I truly believed I could hear a whispered response: "Trust me. Do you trust me?"

I laugh about it now, because instead of being awed by the experience, I just nodded and said: "Sure, I trust you, Lord. So does that mean I can keep my hair?"

Spoiler alert: I lost every single strand several times over, with each round of chemo.

Months later, when my hair began to grow back, it came in silver-white. Not patchy, not curly where it used to be straight, like many cancer survivors experience, but luminous—like a gift. I realized one day, staring in the mirror, that this was yet another glimmer. A very real, tangible one, and my own personal, everyday reminder of God's faithfulness. He hadn't given me what I asked for, but he had given me something better: proof that I could trust him. A visible sign, right on my head, that he could and would always do more than I ask or imagine.

That's what a glimmer is. It's not always obvious, and it's certainly not always what you *ask* for, so if you're too stubborn and set on seeing what you want to see, then you just might not see the gift for what it is. Sometimes the glimmers we find ourselves able to see during times of grief are those entirely unexpected shimmers, those left-field surprises that prove he's listening, he cares, and he provides.

Seek and You Will Find

When I add up everything my family and I went through during those difficult years—the chemo, the hardships, the losses—what

I remember most are the glimmers. I can think back with a smile on those memories and moments that proved God was faithful and present, not just for me, but for the people I love. Because, again, God doesn't have grandchildren. He has a direct, personal relationship with each of us.

I choose to keep a hopeful eye out for God's quiet and good movement through the world. I put on a lens that lets me see his gifts. And I keep my eyes open for the shimmers of iridescence that remind me he is at work, for those moments of unexpected beauty that stop me in my tracks, like the sight of a delicate, intricate spider's web glimmering in an early sunrise. It's so easy to miss those moments, unless you're looking for them.

And I've found that when I look for them, they are always there.

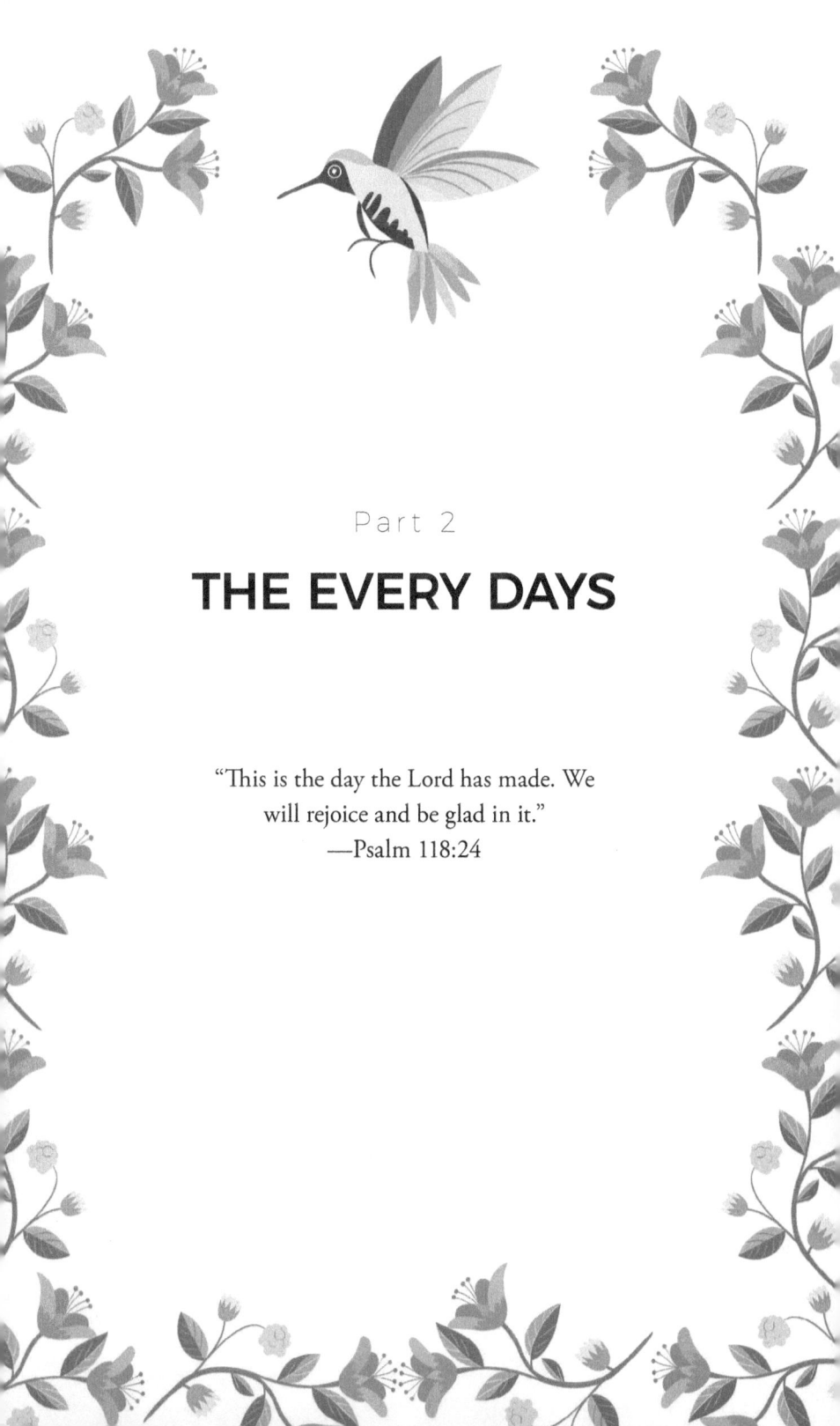

Part 2

THE EVERY DAYS

"This is the day the Lord has made. We
will rejoice and be glad in it."
—Psalm 118:24

Chapter 6

INTENTIONALITY: MAINTAINING GOD'S LENS ON EVERYDAY LIFE

W E'VE EXPLORED THE lenses God gives us during hardship, the lenses that carry us through grief and loss:

- the clarifying focus of tunnel vision
- the compassion and patience that life-and-death experiences can provide
- the freedom of choosing to surrender control
- an acceptance of necessary negative emotions
- the choice to keep our eyes open for God's presence and actions glimmering around us throughout our darkest times

And now we move into the "every days," those long periods that tend to make up the largest part of an average human life, uneventful and mundane and beautiful in their very ordinariness. The "every days" require *work*. They require intentionality.

Life as Usual

I remember experiencing an incongruous feeling of let-down when I came "back to earth," returning to the rhythms of normal life, after beating cancer. Maybe you've gone through something similar, and you know: it's a bit jarring. You've been fully immersed in this place of intense focus and intense faith, and then it's just over. You're no longer in the thick of a life-and-death struggle or resounding heartache that excuses you from focusing on the little non-essentials: team meetings, dinner prep, and paperwork. You have to come back to "real life" after being so absorbed in your own journey, deep in prayer, your faith walk feeling extra special, vibrant, and real because you were resting in the peace of knowing that only God can sustain you.

And then you return, and you lose focus of the fact that God still cares about you *just as much,* as you move through your mundane daily schedule, as he did when you were in chemo, navigating the immediate aftermath of a tragedy, struggling with an emotional health crisis, or whatever your dark times may have entailed.

I know that, for me, the return to daily life was a struggle. I had such a fear of losing the depth of faith that had come during my treatments. I had to learn what it meant to sustain a strong faith and reliance on God during the OK times too.

A Choice You Make Every Day

When that dramatic shift in focus comes during a return to "life as usual," the key is to stay aware and to be intentional.

Intense faith and prayer are no longer the default, a baseline necessity that sustains you. It's relegated to the background again, something you have to work to make time for, something you can easily get by without if other, more real, more pressing demands crowd it out. You have to (with God's help) *choose* it—every single day. You have to make the choice to pray, to read the Bible, and to thoughtfully apply Christ's teachings in everyday life, even if you think you no longer "need" all that quite as much as you did when your world was on fire all around you.

Instead of running as fast as you can away from the tough times, quickly forgetting how deeply intertwined the hardships were with your growing faith, you need to acknowledge the shift that's happening. There is a way to have a deep and rich relationship with God without having to live in the intensity of a life-and-death trial. I promise. I've been there.

My mother set the example in my childhood by reading the Bible to my sister and me at breakfast. Every single day while we were home, even as high school students, Mom would follow up our scripture reading with prayers for and with us. The power of prayer was a focal point in my mother's family—she shared the stories of her maternal grandfather's faithful prayers for future generations. Her grandfather knew the power of prayers for future generations too and set the example for the young eyes of a granddaughter—that was my mom. Our habits of reliance on God impact not just our "every days," but can spark a legacy of faith that we cannot measure.

It all comes down to intentional choices: how you interact with a person you don't really like, how you guide your children through their problems, how you spend your time. It takes staying awake. It takes asking, "God, what do you want me to do? How do I respond in love, when I don't feel it? What do you want me to learn?" every step of the way. It takes time in prayer and studying God's word, the Bible, which is the inspired word of God written for us to know *him* and his plan for humanity.

Intentional, Daily Trust

The genetic component to my family's cancer journey is not limited to those of us who have been diagnosed. My immediate family members have all been tested for and confirmed to be BRCA2 positive, technically indicating the potential for cancers (most likely reproductive) is greater for us than the general population. Knowing this fact has been overwhelming at times. In the past, routine doctor appointments could cause stress—even the smallest pause in the doctor's conversation over bloodwork would increase my heart rate. But now, since I know God is unchanging and I know his faithfulness, I know that I don't need to waste time worrying over what could be. I choose to trust him with all of our futures. I believe if he calls us to continue to walk the cancer journey as a family, he will be with us.

Yet, I had a friend remind me last spring that God is the originator of genetics. He created man with intention and can heal any mutation he has allowed. What a comfort! I have determined to no longer walk in fear with each odd pain or family doctor appointment, and I intentionally and specifically pray for God's mercy and grace over all future generations. I put my faith in Jesus, the Great Physician.

Cultivating a Hunger for God

Maintaining your faith and relationship with God, even during the "every days," begins with shifting your own desires.

If, minus the trigger of extraordinary circumstances, you've found your desire for time with God has subsided? *Just do it anyway.* The desire will follow. Start your day in prayer and Scripture, again and again, and you'll find yourself waking up longing for it.

It is not like a magic trick: open my Bible first thing, and then the remainder of the day will proceed in perfect harmony with my expectations and plans. The discipline that begins the intentional prioritization of time with God in prayer, meditation, and Bible study develops a faith that grows stronger as we begin to attribute the coincidences and fortunate breaks to our God, who cares about the details of life. The same God who created the intricate workings of all creation, from the tiniest spider to the entire galaxy with the sun, moon, and stars (and everything in between), loves *you* and cares about the details of your life. When we spend time with him, we learn to trust his plan and bask in the light of his love without struggling to control life and its outcomes.

God created our brains with neuroplasticity, the ability of the brain to change in structure or function in response to experience. Our brains form pathways of habits and beliefs that grow deeper with habits. Our time devoted to prayer and meditation, along with studying scriptures, is an investment in connection to our Creator to give us a clear lens on our "every days."

As the deer pants for the water, when we kindle a natural hunger for God, for time with our Father, we remember who he is and that he's in control, allowing us to keep our lens focused on surrender, dependence, and gratitude. When we are intentional, doing the diligent work and making consistent choices, we program our hearts and minds to remember that we are only the creations, and that the Creator is in charge of the day. We teach ourselves to keep an eye out for his work all around us, the direction he's pulling us, the silver threads of his presence guiding us forward to bless others and to serve him faithfully.

Choosing to See

God wants to change our perspective, but he doesn't force us. And even when we choose to look at the world through God's eyes, seeing his goodness and light shot through it all, the sight doesn't magically erase the pain. Becoming aware of God's intricate faithfulness doesn't automatically change the diagnosis, undo the loss, or make the mundane days exciting and idyllic. But the glimmers do remind us that God is in it with us. That he's weaving something bigger, something good, even out of broken threads.

I like to picture life like we're all standing inside a room filled with a giant beach ball. Each person in the room is pushed against a different panel of color with a different angle, a different perspective. Depending on where you're standing, you see red, blue, or yellow. Someone else might see something entirely different. But if you shift just slightly, the light catches the next panel of color, and suddenly—everything looks different.

God's faithfulness is evident in our everyday lives. Sometimes the results are so amazing that they capture our attention like the glimpse of the spider-silk, glimmering evidence of his presence, as a way of stepping into our line of sight. Our part is to intentionally choose to look for him.

Chapter 7

A THANKFUL HEART (AND EYE)

DURING TIMES OF great hardship, we learn to look for God's shimmering spider-silk strands, tugging and weaving things together all around us. We develop an eye for the silver linings, the way his love is poured out upon us by our neighbors, the little moments of serendipity that have his fingerprints all over them.

And then we come "back to earth." How can we continue to see that beauty, that divine, even in the "every days?" How can we recapture that keen eye for God-glimmers that can be such a lifeline during grief?

Things are normal again, and our faith requires *work*—not the I-can-control-everything kind of work, but the consistent intention of: "God's got this day too." Much of that work began with relearning how to inhabit the rhythms and chores of the everyday with a lens of gratitude—a willingness to notice God's quiet movement, and the way his love continued to spill out through others even when nothing notably special seemed to be happening at all.

We need a lens of gratitude—because choosing gratitude allows us to find joy and purpose in the quiet, repetitive, seemingly unremarkable periods of our lives.

The Struggle of the "Every Days"

When I think about the times of life that have really encapsulated what a struggle it can be to maintain joy and compassion and gratitude during the chores and most prosaic of days, I think back to when I was parenting littles.

Hoo boy. I will be the first to admit that I am not a good little-kid mom, at least not by nature. It is not something that comes easily to me. I am not the lady who thrives on the baby stage, or even the preschool era. I like it when children can communicate verbally and do a few things independently. When my children were little, it seemed someone was always hungry or needed help with a bathroom visit. In the middle of breakfast, they'd ask, "What's for lunch?" or shout, "Mommy, come wipe me." Oh come on, really? Again?

Having said all that, you'd be right to think that when our family made the decision to homeschool, I was setting myself up for a challenge. It was a time full of such love and beauty, when I learned to look for it, but it also perfectly highlighted the barriers that can prevent us from living fully in those everyday moments: boredom, ingratitude, disengagement, and mental escape.

The only real antidote? Gratitude and intentional presence.

Why Gratitude Matters

I, a self-described "not good little-kid mom," chose to homeschool my little kids, and I would never trade that experience for anything.

The thing that transformed it—from an ordinary experience with the potential to generate chronic frustration, into something indescribably memorable and glowing with warmth and joy and love—was gratitude.

Life can slip by you unnoticed; it can drag on, sharpened by resentment and irritation; or it can be something that is lived in and remembered joyfully. It's all about how you choose to look at it.

I'm not saying that homeschooling wasn't hard. It was, in many ways. But even in the midst of the plans and the worksheets and the squabbles, I knew I was beyond blessed to be able to spend so much time with my kids. I loved our flexible, cozy routines, and I have countless beautiful memories of reading the *Little House* books on the trampoline on a crisp fall day, or upside-down on the couch with all our feet up against the wall, just being together, enjoying a story that sparked the imagination. I remember, in one of those moments, thinking: "This is perfect. This can't last forever. I want to remember this." Eighteen years of childhood is *nothing*. I'm so glad I didn't miss it. I'm so glad God gave me the gift of gratitude and allowed me to see those days as he saw them.

That time spent homeschooling allowed us to know each child individually and to foster an appreciation for the personality differences—humor, learning styles, giftedness, and thoughts. Our few years of learning at home together fostered our bond as a family, and I'm so grateful for that fact, especially when I think about Elayna.

I was able to spend so much time with her when she was young, to build so many precious memories. My kids are all still very close today, we remain close as a family, and we don't have to look back at the times we spent with Elayna during the short span of her life and feel any sense of "Gosh, why didn't we . . . ?"

That's the power of gratitude.

Imperfection and Presence

The nice thing about it all is: life doesn't have to be anywhere *near* perfect for you to see it through a lens of gratitude. Everyday frustrations are real, and negative emotions happen. So how exactly *are* we supposed to feel grateful, even when we're in the thick of it?

For me, it started with choosing to be present anyway, to be present *no matter what*. Mentally present and emotionally present, attuned to the person and things happening right in front of me. I'll tell you. *That* is the only way to really live.

Intentional presence doesn't make things perfect, but it'll help you form bonds, deep relationships that seem to just spring right up out of the cracks of imperfection. My kids certainly didn't always behave angelically throughout their lives. I definitely didn't always parent gracefully. But when I chose to lean in, to listen instead of checking out, to laugh at the spilled milk instead of snapping, those moments became seeds of gratitude.

The barriers to gratitude—boredom, disengagement, irritation—are real, and they're especially tempting for those of us with young children. But presence disarms those barriers, each and every one.

I remember car rides when one of my daughters would talk for the entire thirty minutes without taking a breath. I was tempted to check out mentally. Instead, I made myself stay engaged, and gratitude shifted my perspective: *I got to drive her. I got to hear her heart. I got that window of her childhood. These days are fleeting.*

Again, eighteen years go fast. Gratitude is what makes you see them while you have them. And when we are secure in God's love, we can even see our pain and annoyance differently—as part of the texture of a real, grace-filled life.

Gratitude for the Redeeming Blessings

So, we see life through a lens of gratitude when we choose to stay present to it, warts and all. Sometimes our "every days" are extra, *extra* warty, though—like in the aftermath of loss.

After a tragedy, life returns to seemingly ordinary rhythms, but it feels *different*. How can we keep our eyes open to God's blessings, and our hearts full of gratitude, even during those especially trying, disorienting periods? What redeeming moments might we miss if we aren't watching carefully?

I often say that there are as many layers of grief and loss as there are members of a family. The primary layer when we said goodbye to Elayna was her precious family, her husband Russell and her two preschool children. From the beginning of their marriage, Russell became our son, but of course, we knew him best through the filter of Elayna. After her death, he intentionally included us as her parents in decisions and plans. He assured us that we are his family, and we did the same for him. At our first family vacation with all of the kids and grandkids in July after Elayna's death, we got to know Russell as the fine man that he is—not just as her spouse. God has blessed us with a phenomenal, godly man as the Father of our grandchildren. It was at this time that we began to pray for his future and for him to find a mate and partner to be by his side for the remainder of his life.

The "every days" of a grieving single dad can be tiresome and overwhelming, especially in meeting the constant needs of a two- and four-year-old. Our family determined that we would be there for Russell, whatever it took, and cleared our schedules accordingly. Our weekly routine included a sleepover at Mimi and Pops' house every Thursday after school. Russell thoughtfully included me (and his mom) in the "mom" events at school, which were simultaneously special and emotional. My head and my heart were at odds, in those moments—I felt deep appreciation for being included in a Mother's Day tea party with a cute list of "All about Mimi," while the aches of "why" I was included also produced tears that I choked down with all my might. This can be the essence of daily life after loss, your "new normal," the tension between accepting a changed way of living while still longing for what is gone.

Yet, there is no way to quantify the blessings of our togetherness during that time. We enjoyed just being grandparents—we had fun days and hard days—but we also had consistency: the same menu every time, coloring books, Lego-building, dance parties and bedtime stories. It was a blessing that God provided us with a flexible schedule, allowing us to give our "son" thirty hours each week to not be in dad-mode. This teamwork has produced memories and relationships forged in the deep roots to live life every day, however it comes.

Life presents us with amazing signs of redemption from our losses. If we are aware of those signs, we can celebrate. And sometimes it is so boldly obvious that we simply *must* attribute it to God.

One of these goosebump-inducing times in our family's life came quite recently, in the matching of Russell with a lovely lady from church. As things can go when God is orchestrating life, the timing was perfect. They realized they lived on the same street (on opposite ends, although she did walk her dog past his house). Their lives had only a few degrees of separation—same college, family friends of friends, both faithful followers of Christ who trusted God's plan for their lives. She loves children and has so graciously accepted the strong relationship we have with Russell. She respects and honors Elayna. I absolutely love her—I have been praying for her for a year, and when we first met, we hugged so tightly, a recognition of respect and gratitude that God has brought her into our lives. As if God's work was not obvious enough, her name is Hope (defined as "to have confidence and trust" (*The American Heritage Dictionary of the English Language*, 5th Edition). *Our* Hope.

Thank you, God, for your redeeming blessings that transform life after loss into the most joy-soaked, love-textured of "every days."

Gratitude Is Not Just for Parents

I wanted to quickly make a note: though I've told many stories about motherhood here, gratitude is, of course, not limited to parenting. It can illuminate friendships, marriages, workplaces, church communities—anywhere people live real life together.

The barriers to gratitude are the same, no matter what kind of everyday life you lead: you can fall into disengagement, frustration, or escape (maybe through that miniature screen in your pocket). We can *all* fall into the trap of scrolling our way through conversations, checking out when someone we love is chattering away, or resenting the imperfections of a relationship. Gratitude helps us reframe: "I get to be *here*. I get to love this person. I get to practice patience."

Sometimes we must check our attitudes to avoid the dutiful outlook or performing expectations toward family and friends. Life is an activity that requires participation—stop going through the motions, and just *live*. Whether with a friend, a sibling, a spouse, or a coworker, the choice is the same: be present, be grateful, don't miss it.

Practicing Gratitude

Gratitude is a habit and a choice—it's not just "certain people" that can be grateful. Anyone can make the decision to change their perspective.

Do you know the story of the dog, sitting on the porch and just moaning, till someone comes along and asks why? Well, he's sitting on a nail. Why doesn't he move? It doesn't hurt enough. The moral is, sometimes we are more content to gripe about things than to make a change, or to seek out the good. Pretty silly, isn't it? Why on earth don't we just change our lens on life? Love it or change it, and don't wait for life to be *perfect* before you choose gratitude.

If you feel ready to begin, here are a few simple steps or practices I encourage you to look to:

1. **Shift perspective**: Each day, find one thing to be grateful for (even in your struggles). Reframe daily obligations from "I have to" into "I get to." Obligations are opportunities that someone else would love to have.

2. **Capture anxious thoughts**: Notice when worry tightens your stomach or your chest. Stop, and hand it to God. Completely relinquish every time: "God, I trust you with this." We are not the thoughts we think, but the thoughts we believe. Stop believing the lies of fear that separate you from God's loving care.

3. **Document the "aha" moments**: Jot down when you see God at work, when your perspective shifts, or when beauty peeks through the ordinary. Coincidences are beautiful God-moments. Remember them intentionally—it is a reminder of his faithfulness in the struggling times and facilitates finding him next time.

4. **Share it**: Speak gratitude out loud. Encourage a friend, thank your child, or testify in your small group. Gratitude multiplies when shared. We need to hear your story and your experiences of God's faithfulness and redemption.

Gratitude doesn't erase the bumps and bruises that naturally occur throughout our "every days," but it will certainly help you reframe every moment of this lovely life you lead. It'll help you find the gifts.

I think back to those crisp autumn afternoons on the trampoline, kids tucked under each arm, reading aloud. It wasn't glamorous or perfect, but it felt (and still feels, in my memory) incredibly holy, because we were able to pause and look for God's presence and the love glowing through it all. We were able to appreciate the glimmers.

Don't wait for life to be perfect before choosing a lens of gratitude. If you do, you'll miss it.

Chapter 8

OUR FUTILE, BLINDING NEED TO CONTROL THE ROUGH EDGES

S O, ORDINARY LIFE isn't perfect—no surprise there—
but we *can* and *should* choose gratitude anyway, opening our
eyes to the glimmering threads of God's love and grace shot
through our "every days." And we *can* choose to let go, trusting that
"God's got this" throughout all the little ups and downs, the unexpected twists and turns, the things that don't turn out quite how
we personally—being the best judge of how things ought to be, of
course—originally imagined them.

Because, really, this is the question: who's the boss of your "every
days"—you, or God? When I cling to control, I act as though the
answer is me, and I blind myself to the myriad of possibilities God may
have in mind for my day, my family, my life trajectory. That stubborn,
self-inflicted blindness keeps me from seeing the whole picture, the
many gifts available in my life if I'll only release my expectations and
accept God's great plans. In spite of the reminder of my silvery hair in

the mirror every day, I forget how God's ways are higher than mine, and that he can do more than I can ask or imagine.

Even during the most uneventful times of life, control whispers, "If only things were perfect, then you'd be happy." But there will always be some element of your life that is not exactly "right" (at least, in the world's opinion of what "right" looks like). Gratitude for *whatever God gives you* is what unlocks contentment, not a wild scrambling to make life into something it's not. Paul writes, "I have learned to be content with whatever I have." That doesn't come from smoothing life out into our limited imaginings of "just right," but from trusting God with the rough edges.

Vision Blockers

When you hold too tightly to control, it narrows and darkens your vision. Instead of looking up and out at what God may be unfolding, you look only at what you think you can accomplish and manage. You miss the glimmers of God's better way, because it's not how *you* would do it.

I learned this most painfully after my treatment ended. I've already shared how strange and jarring it was to return to "life as usual" after the drama and intensity of my illness. While I was sick, my faith was *so alive.* I prayed daily not for my will but for God's guidance—"What do you want me to do today?" And he showed up. Every morning felt like borrowed breath, and I leaned on him because I had no choice. But the moment treatment was over, I slipped so quickly back into old patterns: prayer, yes—but followed by that familiar assertion: "Thanks, God. I'll take it from here."

I thought I was regaining control of my life, but really, I was blinding myself (again) to the unbelievable, unexpected, iridescent things that God could do if only I'd let him. Even now, through my continuing "every days," I am still learning what surrender means: stopping to seek God first and believe he will guide, provide, and never be absent.

There are busy weeks at the bakery, especially when we are juggling multiple events and large orders that require logistics and organization. One recent obligation-intense week, nothing was going as I had planned, *even though* I had prechecked the technology that needed to work in order to keep sales going in a smooth and efficient manner. I managed my time well, and I had scheduled and controlled as best I could. But things still didn't run as they should, and I *lost* it. I mean, I threw a fit worthy of a hormonal, adolescent girl. My husband, Bryan, got the brunt of it, and I was too angry and too stubborn to accept help or even suggestions.

It was ugly—and prayer and God were not even on the radar—until he was. As I cried in frustration, I just threw my hands up and got alone to just pray—mainly out of desperation, but then in a position of learning. Why does it always have to get to this point before I finally remember to turn to God and level him with the question: "What am I to do now? I don't see how this is going to work, but it has to work."

With deep breathing and just silence, I began to calm down. I could feel my emotions being released with the thoughts of defeat followed by glimmers of hope, then a clearness of thought, an idea—"Hey, what if I try *this*?"

Now, this scenario may seem like the most trivial thing to you, but in my life at least, the "every days" are much more frequent than the big days. And this is my life of "every days." These moments of learning to absolutely go to God first with the frustrations, confusions, and time-sensitive needs for problem resolution. This simple day of clarity via the detour of fit-throwing and tears has become my motion-activated light (or should I say, e-motion-activated reminder) to *stop*. To just stop and turn to God and ask, "What do I do? What can I learn? Please guide my thoughts and responses."

I need to capture those thoughts and remember that God's plans are always larger, more creative, and more life-giving than our own, even if our firm grip on control keeps us from seeing it.

Before cancer, as I've shared, I was a bit of a performance-oriented Christian. I checked the right boxes, did the "good things," and assumed that if I juggled everything well enough, consequences would be minimal and life would stay steady. That mindset worked, but only until it didn't. Illness shattered the illusion. God began teaching me that life in him is not about how well we perform, but about how well we trust him, and how well we let go.

The hardest part wasn't learning this during cancer—it was carrying the lesson forward with me afterward, on my return to "life as usual." My default was still, again, to perform, to control, to measure outcomes by my effort. Every time I tightened my grip, my vision blurred again.

The Lens of Release

Release is the lens that sharpens and broadens your line of sight. When you choose to surrender control, you suddenly see new angles and colors in your circumstances. God brings textures of grace and opportunity you would've missed if you were still white-knuckling the steering wheel.

For me, my journey with my hair was the most visible lesson in release. Losing it forced me to surrender, and then the beautiful silvery-white that appeared later was just the most beautiful surprise. I stopped merely "showing God" my troubles while still hanging on—I finally let *him* hold them.

The same principle applies to everyday frustrations. When I'm tired or hungry or just grumpy, I *still* want to seize back control. I want to fix the situation my way, right away. But release teaches me to pause: "God, what do *you* want me to see here? What will my limited, controlling perspective cause me to miss? Give me your eyes." Recognizing and then acknowledging my weakness, whatever it is in that moment, opens my heart, soul, and mind to God's strength—for when I am weak, he is strong. I continue to pray for this self-awareness and humility to become my first response, not my desperate last.

Control as a Parent

Parenting exposes our impulse to control like little else, and it complicates and magnifies that need for release and trust. Our compulsion is to protect our children, maximize their lives, manage experiences, and solve their problems. We want smooth paths for our kids, easy friendships, successes that reassure us we're doing things right, but we have to trust God to use whatever happens to our little (and big) ones for their good. It might not *look* or *feel* good, of course. It might be hard, they might learn painfully, but I'm a witness to the fact that God will use every bit of it.

There have been times in my children's lives when disappointments and efforts without positive outcomes tested the bounds of my reliance on God. During my daughter Kailey's senior year, the music pieces for our district's choir auditions were perfect for her range—she practiced diligently, with her eyes set on the goal of being selected for the all-state choir that performs in Austin each February. It was going to be the cherry on top of the proverbial ice cream sundae for a high school music experience that had meant so much.

Then, on the Saturday of the audition, Kailey awoke with laryngitis. Heartbreakingly, she tried every singer and speaker hack she could find to make her voice work—only to have the judge say, "I'm sorry, sweetheart, but this is not going to happen today."

Similarly, my son Nate spent the summer after high school traveling the continent and trying out for junior hockey teams, and he faced rejection after rejection. Eventually, though, he made a team. He packed quickly, found a billet family, then drove to Philadelphia just in time for the season—finally finding a place to belong and keep growing in his sport—only to tear his ACL in the first period of the first game of the season.

When I think back on these seeming misfortunes my children faced, I remember being so mad at God, at the circumstances, at the unfairness of these missed opportunities. But it turned out to be exactly what each of them needed in order to grow as God intended them to grow.

Kailey had the opportunity to represent the state of Texas in another competition (on the same weekend as the original all-state goal) and gained a broader perspective on the drama of high school—trivial in comparison to the immensity of the world and God's plan for her life. Nate's hockey journey was postponed by a year, but his fierce determination earned the respect of his coach, who assisted him in continuing his hockey into the collegiate level. These hardships drew them closer to God and gave them his wider lens. Kailey found people she truly connected to, building deeper and true relationships, while Nate found confidence in overcoming big obstacles to assist him in accomplishing more hard things. God redeemed both situations, one hundred percent. That is where, in hindsight, I am grateful to not have the power of God to change the situations—his redemption is always more than I can imagine during the painful times.

We cannot protect our children from every little wound they'll stumble into through their "every days," either now or later, and nor should we. We grew the most through our own hard times, so why would we deny them the same opportunity? Instead, our job is to simply support and stand beside them, saying, "God is not surprised.

He knows what is happening. What might God be teaching you here?" Just as we must release control in our own lives, we must release control in our children's. They need to feel the textures of life: the discomfort, the disappointment, the scratches and rough patches. These are the very things that deepen them, the places where gratitude and resilience are born.

It hurts to let go. It hurts to watch them hurt. But God has no grandchildren. Our kids need their own encounters with his goodness, not a hand-me-down version of ours. That means letting them walk through life's discomforts so they can find him there. When we, as parents, relax our grip on our children, allowing them to be uncomfortable, to skin their knees, and to fight their own battles, we give them a gift: the gift of a real and textured life, and the opportunity for them to grow confidence in a God who loves them more than we do.

It's a gift we can give ourselves too.

What Texture Teaches Us

Think back over your own life. When have you grown and learned the most—during the smoothest and most peaceful periods, or during the times when you seemed to be just dragging yourself forward (or, perhaps, God was doing the dragging), hitting little snags and scraping up against challenges all along the way?

Picture a pure white piece of paper, smooth and pristine and boring. Now let some shadows leak in, some colors, some texture, some layers. An image takes shape, a beautiful one. Much better, right?

Our everyday discomforts and little pains are what give life depth and texture, what keep life interesting, what make life *life* at all. They keep us awake and alive.

Marriage Adds Dimension and Depth

Marriage, particularly our first year together, certainly provided an opportunity to add texture to life. Here Bryan and I were, two young, idealistic adults with different perspectives developed through our childhoods of nurture and nature. Deeply in love with Jesus and each other, we desired to be in sync through our "happily ever after," but first (we said to ourselves), let's make sure we correct the things we don't like about each other.

We laughingly say now that opposites attract, *then attack*. Bryan (my future-focused visionary) saw flaws in me that he believed could be gently corrected in the first twelve months, so that the remaining seventy years would be smooth. Well. That didn't exactly go as planned. He didn't anticipate the pushback from me (his enthusiastic, strong-willed bride).

I remember the relief of reaching our first anniversary: since my parents divorced when I was young, my fear of failing as a marriage partner was real. Now, more than thirty-five years later, I am grateful for every easy and difficult year of marriage; each provides another layer of depth and texture to our relationship, as well as our perspectives on life and healthy emotional responses. Thanks to God, our marriage covenant continues to be stronger than the ugly (sometimes trivial) conflicts. Through marriage and individual maturity, we continue to uncover past hurts that have created lies we live out. We have learned to call out the reactions that are unreasonable as we relinquish the past to God in our healing process.

Discomforts, conflicts, and the texture they provide are what teach us. They also keep us dependent on the one who guides us through, and they are a part of our process of "becoming," allowing us to stretch and gain wisdom and texture all our own.

That's the beauty of releasing our tight grip on control of the "every days," and of simply accepting them as God gives them to us, minor inconveniences and boredom and all.

Chapter 9

THE ORDINARY AS AN ANCHOR

OF COURSE, AS we've already discussed, life doesn't always maintain an ordinary, tolerable level of discomfort and hardship. Most of us will experience deep valleys interspersed through the long stretches of "every days," and it's during those times that the normal, maybe-boring, sometimes-aggravating moments in life can become a stabilizing comfort.

The Comfort of Normalcy

When crisis hits, it's easy to think life will never feel "normal" again. But so often, in the middle of both my own cancer journey and the losses of my mother and daughter, I found that the ordinary things—the routines, the daily tasks, the small graces of normal life—were what anchored me.

Do you remember being a child, and spinning, spinning, spinning until the whole room whirled around you and you fell flat on your back? We were always told to combat dizziness by keeping our eyes fixed on a static focal point, hoping that steady direction would keep everything from going wonky. It didn't always work, but it usually helped at least somewhat. That's what the daily routines are like, during extraordinary times: stabilizing.

Normalcy brought comfort and gave me purpose. It limited the opportunities I had for self-pity and reminded me that life was still happening all around me, however cramped and urgently focused my own vision had become. Everyday responsibilities broke me out of the myopic tunnel vision that serious illness can create. I want to emphasize again that, yes, that tunnel vision can be clarifying, but you certainly can't live there long-term. You need grounding.

The everyday became that grounding for me.

Anchored by Work

At the time of my diagnosis, I had only owned my bakery for a year, and I know with certainty that God was working all things together for good when he opened the opportunity for me to become a franchisee. I never could have maintained a regular nine-to-five sort of job while seeing the doctor almost daily.

The timing was remarkable: my manager quit right before my diagnosis, but then a young Christian woman who had been an assistant manager contacted me. She could only work for nine months before moving away, so she stepped in to run the bakery through my treatment. When she heard of my cancer, she texted me and said, "God told me to contact you and work for you." I couldn't have orchestrated that if I tried. God knew I needed the bakery to survive—our location was new and needed the benefit of an experienced leader—and more than that, I needed the anchor of a successful business while trusting her leadership.

Even during chemo, I tried to show up at the bakery a couple days a week. Staying connected to everyday life made it harder to slip into a victim identity or to retreat from society. I got energy from my community, and I wanted those around me to catch a glimpse of the hope I was experiencing. It was one way of resisting the temptation to let cancer define me.

The "Every Days" as Identity Keepers

Because looking back, I realize that maintaining the rhythms and experiences of my "every days" during chemo truly did help me protect my identity. I never consciously decided it, but I knew in my gut that cancer was not who I was, that I would not be a victim wearing my survivor label for the rest of my life. Grief was not who I was. Hard things were not my identity. They were just things I was going through. And "going through" implies both a beginning and an end.

That doesn't mean they didn't shape me—they did. But they didn't define me. My identity was (and is) rooted in being God's child. If you learn to see yourself through God's eyes during the little hardships— the textured discomforts of the "every days"—it will be all the easier to remember to keep using that lens during the valleys too. I'll say it again: we are *not* defined by our sorrows. We are not victims. I am a child of God. You are a child of God. That truth is an anchor in itself.

Anchored by Others' Everyday Acts

Some of the most anchoring moments during that season came through the small, everyday kindness of others. I have such a sweet spot in my heart as I remember the little things that kind people did to keep me grounded in my worst moments.

The day Elayna died, a friend asked what I needed from the grocery store. All I could think of was cheese and crackers, and she showed up at my door not long afterward holding a box of Triscuits and a packet of American cheese. Another sweet friend came with toilet paper, paper plates, snacks, and juice boxes, just in case the grandkids were around.

On Christmas Eve, ten months after Elayna died, a woman I had only recently met showed up at my door with a beautiful gift bag of comfort items: cozy socks, a bath bomb, pampering, self-care items like that. She was my dentist's wife—I'd let her husband know about Elayna's passing during a dental cleaning just the day before—and we became instant friends. I didn't even know her first name until that day. I was blown away by her efforts—I mean, it was Christmas Eve. But she said something that changed my perspective: "There are some things more important than what we had planned." Her everyday kindness became an anchor of grace in my grief. Her message of love for me and what I was experiencing continues to resonate when I encounter others in pain. I desire for my anchor, my identity, to be the flexibility of life that allows me to be used when God needs me to show love to others.

Letting Others Anchor You

Many things from my childhood have given me depth of appreciation and vision for others, because of the kindness I received. Growing up in a single-mom household in a small town, I felt safe and protected—we had many caring neighbors who looked out for us. There was an overflowing, kind awareness of our needs, as well as anonymous provision for those needs, that showed respect for my mom's hard work. When a home fire destroyed our laundry room and clothes dryer, the volunteer fire department rebuilt our room, and an anonymous, generous neighbor left a new clothes dryer in our garage. When I needed a formal dress for a school opportunity but had no budget, the local boutique called to let us know that someone had purchased a gift card in my name. Once again, we were grateful for the generous people who stepped up to provide for others—an example I try to honor whenever possible, remembering my own gratitude to God for providing beyond comprehension. In hard times of life, sometimes we are the recipient and sometimes we are the giver—either way, God shows up in the community that believes in his tangible presence.

These experiences taught me that vulnerability is not weakness. If you're going through hardships yourself, I want to encourage you to lean into the anchor of "normal life" by allowing yourself to ask those around you for help, even with the most basic and mundane things. When people ask, "What can I do?" give them something to do. Let them bring over those groceries. Let them write the card. It helps you *both*. Their everyday faithfulness connects you back to normal life, to community, and to God's provision. And once you've received it, you carry that gratitude forward. You begin to look for opportunities to be someone else's anchor later on, down the line. What's *their* Triscuits and American cheese? What small thing can you offer to remind them they're not alone? Don't wait for an answer from the person you're trying to support, because sometimes, in the hardest seasons, we are not sure what we want at all, or struggle to verbalize it. Instead, imagine what *you* might need in their situation, and do that. Whether you hit the bull's-eye or not, your thoughtful actions will be appreciated.

Gratitude for the Everyday

When your life is interrupted by grief or challenge, you realize the value of the "every days." Going to the store, hugging your child, sitting in a meeting, even cleaning the house—these things are blessings. When I was immune-compromised, I couldn't take part in so many of them. Coming back, I felt a fresh appreciation for ordinary privileges I once overlooked.

The ordinary times in your life will not erase pain when the extraordinary times hit, but they can anchor you, ground you, and keep you from drifting into despair or self-pity. And when you learn to see things through the lens of gratitude, the everyday becomes not just background noise, but one of God's greatest gifts.

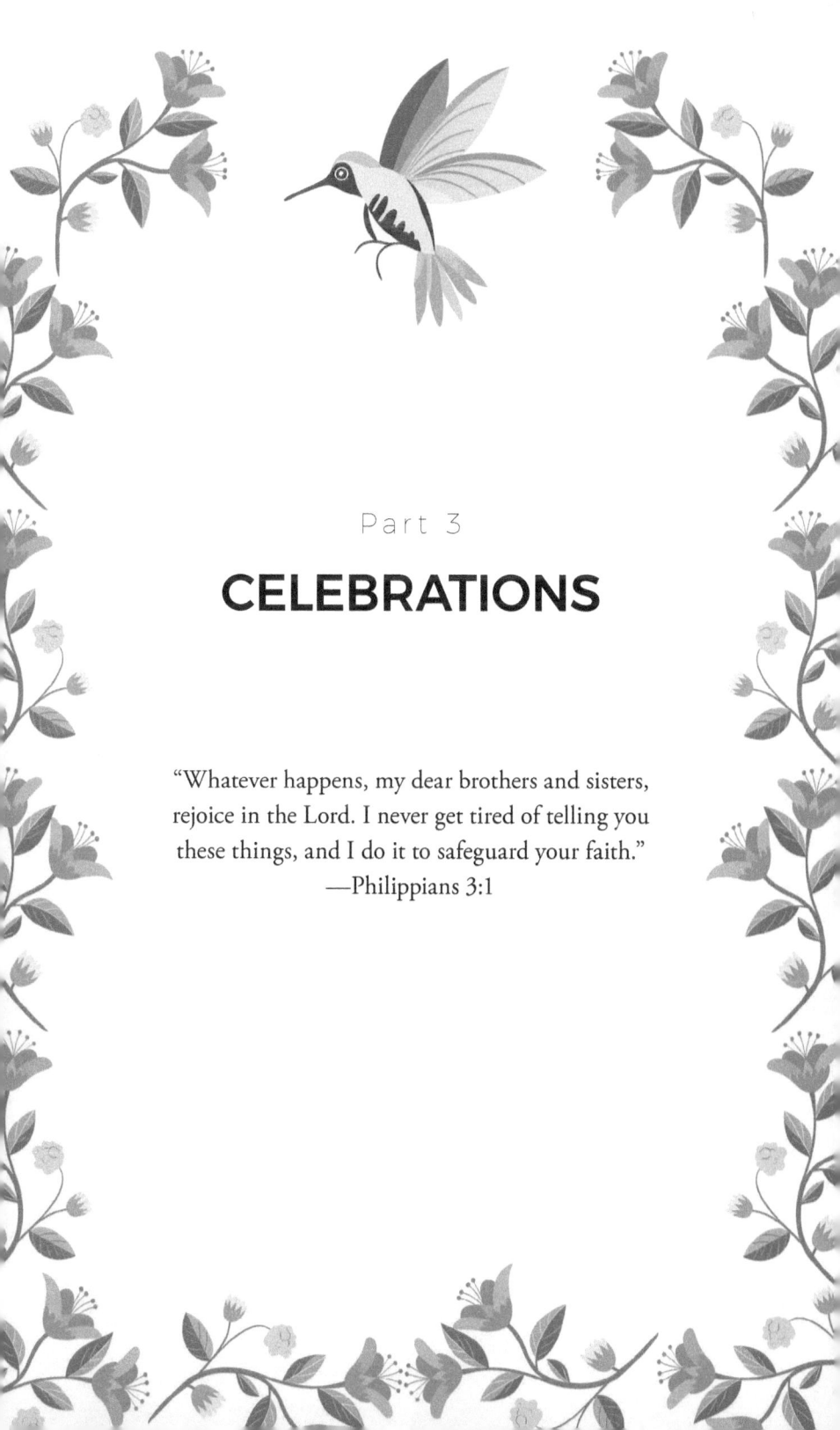

Part 3

CELEBRATIONS

"Whatever happens, my dear brothers and sisters,
rejoice in the Lord. I never get tired of telling you
these things, and I do it to safeguard your faith."
—Philippians 3:1

Chapter 10

PUTTING THE FOCUS ON WHAT MATTERS

D URING TIMES OF great grief, God gifts us many lenses: focused tunnel vision, patience and compassion, surrender, emotional acceptance, and an eye for his iridescent glimmers of loving action all around us.

During the long, textured "every days" too, we can choose, with God's help, to maintain a lens of deep faith; we can carry a brightening perspective of gratitude with us, transforming "boring" into "beautiful"; we can shake off the blinders of our own stubborn impulse to control the little discomforts that give life its texture; and we can return to the beauty we find in those threads of normalcy, allowing it to anchor us during our darkest times.

As we increase in our appreciation for that anchoring quality of our "every days," rough edges and all, our gratitude for the small and commonplace things naturally spills out into how we celebrate.

Appreciating the "Little" Celebrations

When we think of celebrations, we usually think of the big ones first: weddings, graduations, birthdays, Christmas. Those aren't the only ones that matter, though. I want to start by talking about the little ones. The mini-celebrations are the family gatherings that happen for next to no reason, yet swell with joy and togetherness. Sometimes it's just a shared brownie and a bowl of ice cream, or an afternoon of laughing together, swimming, and eating watermelon, that reminds us just how precious life and love truly are.

I grew up with my mom, but remained very close to my dad's family. I *still* appreciate Sunday afternoons watching football with my uncles. My grandma's fried chicken, fresh garden vegetables, and fluffy homemade biscuits after church provided the initial draw. My uncles and grandpa taught me rules, strategies, and terminology of football, as well as the release of yelling at a television in frustration—things that I continue to share with my kids and grandkids. Such ordinary yet special and bonding times. God provided an enduring connection to my extended family through these days. Whatever a celebration or gathering may look like, formal or informal, planned or spontaneous, those moments matter.

Even when they change.

Family times after Elayna's death felt muted for a while. The depth of humor and unique perspective she brought to our time together was obviously missing. But over time, we realized her presence lingered on in how we continued to see things, as well as in our memories, inside jokes, and shared phrases. It reminded me to savor the fact that we prioritize making time to be *together* as a family. The purpose of our celebration was nothing more than that: intentional togetherness, intentional presence.

It only takes interacting with one lonely person to remind you how blessed you are that God has provided you with family around you. Times like those are priceless. They provide a window into how *everything may change*, but God's presence is there, even in the transitional, bittersweet times.

Celebrate by Being Present

Something funny happened at one of our recent family gatherings. All the grown men in our family—big, strong men, one and all—decided to cannonball into the pool one after the other—rocking the waves out of the pool. The water exploded everywhere, with grandkids giggling and trying to figure out how to splash that high. It was so fun and so crazy, and my husband shouted to my daughter, "Go get the camera!"

But Kailey just shook her head. "Nah. I don't want to get out of the pool." She stayed, got splashed, and *experienced* that moment.

Not everything has to be documented. Some celebrations are best seared into memory, not viewed from a distance through the lens of a phone camera. (Although, sure, I'm not begrudging anyone their photos of memorable moments and milestones—I actually wish I remembered to take photos more often.) Presence enhances celebration. It's like watching a game live instead of on TV—being *there* changes everything.

What's Worth Celebrating?

Those little celebrations matter because of what they entail: togetherness, attention, deliberate time lovingly spent. Those are good reasons to congregate, to celebrate. But so-called celebrations can ring hollow, too, when they happen for every reason.

Our culture pushes us to make everything into a capital-E Event. I'm talking about kindergarten graduations, monthly baby photoshoots, first-day-of-school rituals. My grandkids and I were watching neighbors stand out in their driveways recently, taking "back to school" photos, and my grandson asked me, "Wait, *why* do they want a photo of them just going to school?" It's a good question. Sometimes the most marketing-inspired, culturally-created celebrations are fun (and there's nothing wrong with enjoying them), but I'm of the mind that if everything is a party, nothing is. We need to ask why. *We need discernment.*

This reminds me of the old story of the young married lady who cut the end of the roast off each time she placed it in the pan to be cooked in the oven. Her husband asked one day why she cut the end off—it looked like a perfectly good cut of meat. She said her mom has always cut the end off, so that is what you do. Then she asked her mom why *she* cut the end off, and the answer was similar: "My mom always did it. Hm, I wonder why. Let's ask Grandma." Grandma said, "Oh dear. My oven and pan were smaller than the average cut of roast, so I always had to cut it to make it fit in the pan."

There may be many activities that fall into the category of "that's just what you do" that may not make sense or have meaning for your family at all when examined with a critical eye.

What really matters to your family? Does this celebration line up with who God's calling you to be? Are you doing it because it resonates, or because Instagram says you should? Prayerful discernment makes our celebrations meaningful, not empty. If it's not centered on what really matters to you and yours—for example, faith, family, love—then *why on earth are you doing it*? Major holidays may become frantic checklists—expensive and exhausting. Instead of giving in to the pressure, determine what is a meaningful tradition for *you* and for *your family*—I would encourage you to focus on the relationships and time together, versus the "things" and schedules. Most of our memories are people-centric, in the end, and God can give you discernment to enjoy what is heartfelt without the need for perfection and post-worthy experiences. Make your plans, but then release the outcome and simply enjoy. *Whatever* you do, consciously analyze your motives and craft your celebrations with intentionality.

Then, and only then, can you trust your celebrations to turn your eyes back toward what really matters, to give you a hopeful and joyful lens on life while creating memories for generations to come.

Rhythms of Remembrance

The world has rhythms, and the church does too. There's beauty and power in our cycles of celebration. Some of our celebrations point us forward, but many of them also encourage us to look back and to remember. The Bible is full of reminders from God to remember him and what he has done.

I've been reading the New Testament in light of the Old Testament lately, and have really been enjoying learning more about the celebrations God put in place for the ancient Israelites. He knows how easily we forget and move mindlessly on from thing to thing. That's why he built celebrations into the rhythm of his people—Passover (Exodus 12:6–11; 24–27), the stones of remembrance by the Jordan (Joshua 4:1–7). We take communion in remembrance of Jesus (Luke 22:19). We have to be intentional about remembering all the times God has been faithful and celebrate all that he has done.

When you're faced with a life-and-death situation, it really does shake things down to their core, returning you to your motivations. It's hard to return to doing things "just because" once you find your feet back on solid ground, because you are forever changed, your lens shifted, your perspective reset. I thank God for that transformed lens he gave me, because it allows me to let celebrations be what they should be: meaningful, focusing, comforting, and clarifying. When we celebrate with intention—whether it's a french fry taste test, a BBQ for no reason beyond being together, or a specific holiday—we're setting our eyes back on what matters most.

Chapter 11

GATHER THE GLIMMERS, COLOR THE DAYS WITH HOPE

I DON'T WANT YOU to think I'm disparaging or belittling celebrations—not by any stretch of the imagination. I just want to affirm their true meaning and intent, and insist that celebrations don't have to look a particular way, in line with any cultural, social media-fueled norms, to do what they're meant to do: clarify our vision around what truly matters.

Celebrations Happen with Those You Love

Some celebrations, as we've explored, are small, informal gatherings (no less imbued with love and intentional meaning because of their size or informality, though). Others mark big milestones—weddings, graduations, birthdays—that deserve serious intentionality.

These moments are often future-focused, hopeful, and designed to proclaim: life has meaning, life is worth supporting, life has hope for the next season.

Strangers don't celebrate your milestones with you. *Your people* do. It's an honor to be invited to someone's wedding, birthday, or graduation, because they're showing you they want you there, supporting them. It's not just a party. It's not just about showing up for the free food and alcohol. It's about being there with the ones you love. That's why milestones matter. Not for the photos or the decorations, but for the community of love and support that shows up.

Each of our children's marriages was a beautiful time of celebration. As they grew up, our prayer for them was always that God would prepare the hearts of their future spouses, and for their marriages to make them stronger Christ-followers. Our prayers were answered. Their weddings were lovely, worshipful services that honored God, followed by personalized parties that represented each couple in a unique way. Love and laughter echoed among our extended family and created a new family with joy in the sanctity of marriage to honor the Lord. He was present at each union.

One of the most inspiring moments took place at our son's wedding. His wife, Courtney, is one of the most thoughtful people ever, so every intentional detail was deliberate. All four sets of their grandparents were able to attend this special day—as you can imagine, with an average age of 80, mobility was a bit challenging for most of them. Courtney arranged for all of them to arrive early to have a special "first look" with her. The facial expressions of love and awe are indelibly marked in my memory. My daughters and I could barely contain the tears as we witnessed her grandparents and Nate's grandparents hug her and each other in this oh-so-special moment. What makes it even more remarkable is that within a year, three of those eight legendary examples of marriage (almost two hundred years of marital experience) had gone from this earth to spend eternity with Jesus. I am thankful God allowed that blessed gathering, and we share warm memories of that most historic moment.

Milestones are meant to be celebrated with those you love. When I think back on my own wedding, I can see that truth in vivid color.

It was the 1980s, so there were no cell phones or curated social media feeds. Some of my friends brought a Polaroid along, snapped all kinds of photos throughout the ceremony and reception, and then cut them out and put them in a wallet-sized photo book to hand us as we drove away that very day, saying only, "We want you to remember this while you are on your honeymoon." What a simple, thoughtful act. It's stayed with me throughout the decades, and I truly believe God placed people like that in my life to teach me how to love. I remember my mom just beaming, relishing the whole event, and talking about how there's nothing like a wedding for the love of a community to show up. Goodness, was she right.

Celebrations like these are a shimmering lightshow of God's iridescent glimmers, where the starbursts and rainbows of love and joy all coalesce and color life for days to come. What a blessing. What a grounding. What a perspective.

Celebrations Point Us Forward with Hope

So many of our celebrations are about supporting something *new*: a new couple, a new family, a new age, a new era. I remember the mixed emotions of ringing the bell after successfully completing my cancer treatment. Hope was definitely one of those layers, an especially bright thread, shining as silver-white as my new hair.

Traditions are great ways to look forward with hope, while also reminiscing. One tradition we have as a family is an annual vacation with Bryan and me, the kids, their spouses, and all of the grandchildren.

This began three years ago, when we had so much fun at the beach celebrating Mom's birthday.

The next year, we returned to the beach. We shared cooking duties, played games when the kids were in bed, romped on the beach, and took turns holding the littles in the waves (some more easily than others). We began making great memories, but the drive or flight was quite cumbersome, so we changed to Table Rock Lake, Missouri. We have been to the same family-oriented resort for several years now, and the memories are already multiplying. I enjoy the laughter, activity, and echoing footsteps through the cabin—it takes some logistics to sleep kids, infants, and adults in a fashion that is somewhat private, yet not stifling to others. The pool time, porch time, s'mores, and fireworks fill many of the memories.

This year, I made the announcement that we would probably go to a biannual vacation versus an annual one, as our young families have limited vacation time, and we were allocating five to seven days of that time to this commitment. (Also, some of the grandchildren get carsick in the mountainous portions of the drive, so I thought this may be creating a less-than-memorable time for them.) I believed each family would like the freedom to have their own family vacation or join friends. It was my way of "letting them out" of the obligation.

But the kindest interaction happened with one of my sons-in-law on the last trip. He asked, "Why are we not doing this again next year? Why are we waiting?" I shared my thoughts, and everyone chimed in, "No; we love this time together."

I had underestimated the joy of being all together with individual conversations and the communal feel of helping with the kids and life. We will resume this annual tradition. The importance of the tradition has been reinforced by the grandkids as they begin conversations with "Remember when we . . . at Table Rock?" I look forward to *years* of memories on vacation with the whole family at Table Rock Lake with anticipation and joy.

Our milestones, and the imperfect, love-filled celebrations that accompany them, propel us forward into whatever comes next with hope. They gather the glimmers, infuse life with gratitude, and cast the light of hope out before us as our feet faithfully follow.

Chapter 12

HOPE AND CONTINUITY

B ECAUSE THAT, REALLY, is what celebrations are all about: hope. (Not that *Hope*—God's.)

Celebrations point us back, reminding us of God's faithfulness. They point us forward, coloring our futures with hope. They are warmed and sanctified by love and presence and intention, and they remind us of what really matters.

Sometimes the hardest place to do *any* of those things, though, is in the dark.

And yet, the valley is *exactly* the place where God's people have always found reasons to rejoice. Some of that comes from our confidence that God will continue to be faithful, that there are plans that are higher than ours, and that worlds exist beyond what our eyes can perceive, continuing even beyond the sting of death. As believers, too, these celebrations are an opportunity for us to lean into our unique understanding and hope in life's continuity, of a joyous existence with God beyond the bounds of this world.

But we also, quite simply, trust that God will be faithful—*whatever* that faithfulness may look like.

The ancient Israelites marked their calendars with feasts that echoed stories of God's deliverance—Passover reminding them that he brought them out of slavery in Egypt (Exodus 12:6–11; 24–27), Purim reminding them he protected them from destruction (Esther 9:20–28), the stones by the Jordan reminding them that he made a way through the waters (Joshua 4:1–7), and for Christians today, communion regularly to remember Christ's sacrifice for our sins (Luke 22:19). Each celebration carries this dual purpose: to remember what God had already done, and to affirm that he will show up again.

Celebration lights up the darkness. It reminds us we are not abandoned, that God is faithful, and that heaven is real.

Living with Heaven in Mind

How do you celebrate your birthday when you know it may be your last?

My cancer biopsy was scheduled right on my birthday, as it happens, so I was ill, but didn't know it yet (at least not for sure). By the time my next birthday came around, I had already come all the way through the diagnosis and out the other side, so I never actually experienced a birthday while in the midst of treatment. I didn't have to ponder my own mortality on a day meant to celebrate my life, but that brush with death *did* change how I celebrated moving forward. Each cake and candle became an act of defiance against despair, a way of saying, *No matter what happens, this life is not all there is. I am anchored in hope. This earth and body are not my forever home.*

Oh boy: after my cancer, my mom's, and my daughter's, my whole family has become heavily familiar with the cancer fight, and with questions of life and death. In some ways, our experiences have given us a kind of telescope that lets us look past the hard stuff of the "here and now," the problems of sin and decay in the human body, and toward the fact that this earth is not our home. We were made for life with Jesus. That knowledge can add to our celebrations, and it can lead us to say: "This is where I am for now, and I'm not going to take it for granted. Let's continue to celebrate, no matter how many days we may have left." That's such a helpful perspective, one that allows for deep gratitude, hope, maximized moments, and no regrets—no matter what path our lovely, numbered days may take.

When I rang the bell at the end of my cancer treatment, my emotions were so layered. Gratitude, yes—but also empathy. Because I knew in the next room, someone else would never get to ring the bell. For me, that particular celebration was simply saying, "I am here, instead of in heaven. Both are good. But God has given me this day, and I will use it for good."

Choosing Worship over Despair

When Elayna and my mom were each sick, we made the most of every celebration, and especially maximized the informal events—like the partial eclipse, a first for all the grandkids with their parents. Game nights and spontaneous dinners became bright, colorful, and unforgettable. Looking back on them, I have no regrets at all.

Even Paul and Silas sang hymns in prison (Acts 16:25–26). In the face of persecution, they chose worship over despair. That's what celebration can be. A discipline of hope, a lens that looks past the tunnel of suffering to the light ahead.

We can do the same by choosing life and light and togetherness, even when death and darkness loom.

When we arrived to celebrate my mom's eightieth birthday at the beach, months before she passed away, she hugged me so tightly and whispered, "I already love this so much that we're all together. I can never thank you enough." It wasn't the location, plans, or food that mattered so much. It was just about being together. It was memory-making that outlasted all the hard things, in this world and beyond.

Celebrations of life are like that too. You feel joy for those who've preceded you to live with the Father, and the sharpness of missing them, and you're reminded of what truly matters. Happy and sad tears mix together to blur your vision. Grief and gratitude become hard to tell apart, but in the mix, there are glimpses of heaven, glimpses that remind you that God's presence and our spiritual, eternal souls are not bound by time as our physical bodies are. Our loved ones, in a way that is not explainable, are merely "in the next room" with Jesus. We will see them again.

God's Light in the Dark

It may be hard to understand when I say this, but the greatest peace I've ever known came the day we buried Elayna—her celebration of life service.

That day, I gave no thought to details, outcomes, clothes, or appearances. I was a vessel being used by God, comforting others, radiantly sharing God's love with all who attended. It was worship, prayer, miracle—the most peace-filled day of my entire life. The Holy Spirit was present throughout the whole day. Much later, I shared that with a young dad who had also buried his child. He said, "I felt the same way, but I've never told anyone. I felt guilty." It was a good reminder for us both: there is nothing unnatural about feeling peace at someone's passing into the arms of Jesus. It is God's peace—the peace that exceeds all we can understand. Peace like that is a gift meant to be shared. What other experience can give us that long view, that eternal and comforting perspective?

Even in funerals, we celebrate because God is faithful. Earth is not our home. Celebration keeps our eyes lifted, reminding us that life continues, that eternity is real, that we are safe in his hands.

Choosing the Lens of Hope

That truth shifts how I celebrate, because there is no fear in God. Instead of asking, "Why is this happening to me?" and allowing the everyday moments and celebrations to be robbed of joy, I've learned to ask, "Lord, what do you want me to learn from this?" That reorientation frees me from despair. It reminds me that Satan would love nothing more than for me to live afraid and anxious—but God calls me to *joy and hope*. Again, even Paul and Silas, chained in prison, chose hymns. I can choose too.

Nothing represents that choice quite as well as when my son and I participated in the BMW Annual Dallas Marathon together—an idea that God put on my heart after Elayna's death. I thought it would help Nate and me get moving again, emerging from the sedentary phase of grieving the death of his sister and my daughter. I also believe, now, that God was giving all of us something to accomplish together, something we could then *celebrate* together.

I invited my family to participate in the marathon in memory of Elayna, because I had only ever run one half-marathon before, and that had been with Elayna, ten years earlier. Both my son and his wife, Courtney, decided to join. Nate trained for the ultramarathon (thirty-one miles) and Courtney trained to run her first half-marathon through the fall. The common goal kept us all accountable as I prepared for my walking half-marathon. Eventually, Nate and Courtney revealed they had a larger challenge in mind—to raise money for cancer research to honor Elayna's memory. They researched an organization that they learned about through a genetic counselor, and the Elayna Rogers Johnson Memorial Marathon Fundraiser was established. Nate's tribute was heartfelt and such a beautiful testament to their relationship. He set a large goal for the fundraising without focusing on the amount, but on the cause. The outpouring of generosity from across our lives was humbling and inspiring.

We continued to train and plan. Kailey found a way to get one of Elayna's fabric designs produced so we could adorn our race-day attire in some way to include Elayna's artistic contribution in the actual race. On marathon eve, after packet pick up and a note on the participants' banner signifying our cause, we began decorating our gear: me adding the sporty floral print to my cap brim, Courtney embellishing her top with heart cut-outs and Nate sewing the fabric over one of his sleeves.

Race morning was humid; mist and gloom hung in the air as we waited to race, each in our separate corrals. We were all melancholy in our purpose all day through the rain and mist, potholes and hills. I listened to my worship playlist as I always do when I walk—this list was particularly full of Elayna memories from her cancer-battle months to her celebration of life worship songs.

Nate was also very contemplative, and each of us shed tears in our hours alone on the course. Nate was pleased with his pace when a family member caught up with him at mile twenty-two, so we waited at the finish line and tracked his progress on the racing app. The whole family was there waiting for Nate to finish. As he reached the last hundred yards, *he began to sprint.* The emcees of the race who were calling out finishers, "Nate Rogers of . . . wait, is that Nate Rogers? Wow! Way to go. Nate, what a powerful finish!" The announcer has no idea of the depth and truth of his word choice. There were no dry eyes in the Rogers crew as we witnessed this truly God-empowered finish.

This is just exactly what it was: a powerful finish to his tribute to his sister, one of the biggest influences in his life. A powerful finish is how Elayna lived her final months in her earthly body. A powerful finish because the final push to promote the ERJ Memorial Fundraiser resulted in 33 percent more donations than the goal. As we looked back at pictures of the day, we realized that the shirts of another group gathered to celebrate their marathon finish read: "Blessed are those who mourn, for they will be comforted" (Matthew 5:4). Thank God for yet another God-wink in this glorious path of processing, grieving, and growing.

God used that marathon in our lives to allow each of us to organically contribute, process, share and heal as individuals and as a family unit. Through Nate's powerful finish, in particular, he allowed us to *celebrate* together and to remember Elayna's own powerful finish as she crossed the finish line of her earthly life.

Celebrations can happen, powerfully, transformatively, even in the midst of tragedy. If you can't see the light at the end of the tunnel, it doesn't mean it's not there. Turn your face toward God's light, not the shadows behind you.

The Source of All Light

In the end, God is the source of every glimmer of light we see through *any* lens we wear. John 1:5 says, "The light (Jesus) shines in the darkness, and the darkness can never extinguish it." He is the one who makes funerals become worship services, who turns birthday candles into acts of defiance against despair, who transforms cannonballs in the pool or a quiet hug at the beach into sacred remembrances.

Celebration is all about hope and about continuity. It's lifting our eyes above the brokenness of today and choosing to proclaim:

God has been faithful before, he is faithful now, and he will be faithful forever.

We can keep our eyes on the glimmering iridescence. We can see the good that can only be from God. James 1:17 tells us, "Whatever is good and perfect is a gift coming down to us from God our Father, who created all the lights in the heavens. He never changes or casts a shifting shadow."

Chapter 13

CONCLUSION

FRIENDS, AS YOU wrap up your reading of this book, I want to leave you with a few final reminders.

You've walked with me through my family's story, and (I hope) have absorbed some of the lessons I learned around the lenses we encounter during all the seasons of our lives:

- God gives us a narrowed focus during times of crisis, revealing his presence and provision in the urgent.
- Hardship teaches us empathy and patience, giving us a grace-filled perspective that keeps the little things little.
- God alone sees the whole picture, and we cannot orchestrate the feelings or experiences of others. He will redeem what he allows, and his redemption is beautiful.
- Every emotion has value, and we must accept them all in order to live life in "full color." Sometimes it is blended altogether—the positive and the negative in an emulsive state.
- God's faithfulness always shines through, and we can see the glimmers if we only choose to look.

- We can maintain the lens God gives us during tragedy, carrying it with us into the "every days," through consistent intentionality. His faithfulness is the same no matter our circumstances.
- Gratitude can transform and hallow our view of even the most mundane and ordinary times of life.
- Clinging to control and attempting to erase the little discomforts that give life its texture will blind us to God's imaginative possibilities for our (and our children's) lives and days.
- Ordinary rhythms can give us a grounding, a point of stabilizing focus, during seasons of loss or illness. Kindness is always a good idea. Whether you are comfortable or not, be obedient to the nudge of action to show you care. Be a good kindness-giver and receiver.
- Celebrations help us refocus on what really matters (with intention, presence, and surrounded by those we love).
- True celebrations allow the glimmers to coalesce and shed light over the surrounding days.
- When we celebrate with an eye on the whole, eternal scope of a human life—in earthly life and the life beyond—we gain a lens of anchoring hope.

A Final Encouragement

I don't have hope because I was ordained to be hopeful. Each of us is offered the perspective of hope through God's love. We can find the good in any situation with the right lens. In Matthew 7:8, Jesus tells us, "Everyone who seeks finds..." Every single one of us has the opportunity and the *choice* to take on God's lens—to see his light and presence and faithfulness all around us throughout our seasons of grief, the "every days," and the times of celebration alike.

This is an opportunity for those of us who accept the love of God to live a life of hope, peace, and joy.

A vibrant life despite circumstances attracts others in curiosity, like a moth attracted to the light. When they ask why we have hope, we have an opportunity to show them God's love through the truth of our experiences. (As Peter puts it, "Instead, you must worship Christ as Lord of your life. And if someone asks about your hope as a believer, always be ready to explain it.")

Imagine the powerful floodlight we can shine in the dark world when we see and share things through God's lens of hope. That is something that every one of us can do, regardless of our circumstances, by taking on a lens that lets us see God's glimmers, and by learning to approach whatever life throws our way with a few thoughts:

- "God, what do you want me to learn from this?"
- "How can I keep praising you, no matter what?"
- "Will you help my unbelief? I don't want to live in fear."
- "I trust you, Lord. You redeem all things."

With God guiding and supporting you, I pray you'll step into hope and joy anew. Look for good—you will discover God.

A Final Prayer

Dear Heavenly Father,

I pray for your blessing on the lives of all who read and hear this book. I pray that the reality of your unchanging love will resonate in the souls of the hurting and discouraged with healing and truth.

As we walk through grief and loss in this broken, fallen world, may we not get stuck in the sadness or disappointment of lost futures and expectations. May we turn toward your light of hope, promise and redemption.

You have not promised us easy lives as your children, but you have promised that we are not alone. You are with us. May we also be together in community for and with each other. Cheering, loving, encouraging and supporting each other as a family—through grief, the "every days," and in celebration.

May we continue to grow in our understanding of your great love for us and in our belief in the truth of your goodness.

May this book be a dew drop on the glistening web that is this life, sparkling with an iridescent beauty that can only be attributed to you—the Creator of everything, and the author of every good and perfect gift.

In Jesus's name I pray.
Amen.

ACKNOWLEDGMENTS

THANKS TO MY Lord and Savior, Jesus Christ: his life brought light to everyone. The light shines in the darkness, and the darkness can never extinguish it (John 1:4–5). May we see more clearly through him.

Thank you to the team at Streamline: Hallie, Marcie, and Alex. This experience has been easier because of your guidance and leadership. I appreciate you so much.

Thank you to Kathryn and Jon Gordon and the whole team at Gordon Publishing and Jon Gordon Companies. Your confidence and belief in me have given me the courage to complete this book. I can't imagine doing this with anyone else. Thank you for believing in me.

Thank you to my Courageous Moms, New Hope, Bundt Babes and COR communities for being the hands and feet of God through serving, praying, providing food, hugs, and kindness. I could never thank you enough for everything you have done for me and my family over these years.

My friends, RK, MK, AW, and MG. Our friendships are based in our Lord, and no matter what time passes, I always know you are there for me and my family until we are all home with Jesus.

My family—your support for me is humbling and outrageous. Your support is always exactly what I need—however that looks, and it has looked pretty silly at times. I get overwhelmed with emotion at the blessings you have all been in my life. Thank you for everything.

Elayna, Mom, Charles, Nell, and Uncle Bubba—we'll get there as soon as we can, or see you as soon as Jesus comes back.

Sisters know without words—thank you, sister. You truly are the genius in the family.

Kailey, Robert, Archer, Sydney, Clara and Baby Boy, Russell, Hope, Wesley, and Lottie, Nate, and Courtney—I am honored to be your galvanizer and to spend every important moment of my days with you. I am beyond proud of the godly, caring people that each of you is. Thank you for loving me, loud laughter and all. I have learned so much from you—you are my inspiration. TeamRogers, 4-ever. TARRAANR I love you all.

BR: Thankfully, I can't imagine life or who I would be without you. The years of growing with you are the best. Thank you for believing in me when I didn't believe in myself—you have always been the visionary of our family, with your focus pointing us to Jesus. Thank you for leading us all. I love you.

ABOUT THE AUTHOR

Kathy Rogers is a speaker, consultant, Nothing Bundt Cakes franchisee, podcaster—and now author—whose life was forever changed by two potentially devastating breast cancer diagnoses—first her own and then her daughter's. While she earned accolades for strong business accomplishments, Kathy's most profound journey began in her faith when cancer entered her family's story.

Her personal experience of faith, joy, and perseverance took on new meaning when her daughter was diagnosed with breast cancer at a young age. Despite the fierce battle, Kathy's daughter passed away at just twenty-nine years old, leaving behind her husband and young family. This unimaginable loss transformed Kathy's focus of pain and loss to one of seeing and trusting God, which continued to grow her faith, joy and peace. Living with an emphasis on finding good, while knowing God is good and he will redeem all he allows in this precious life.

Through her involvement in national advisory boards, nonprofit organizations, and faith-based communities—whether leading a retreat or workshop or sharing an inspiring message of hope in God's love, Kathy has found purpose in her journey to encourage others to discover the same God who created the universe cares about the details of our lives. Her engaging personality and honest approach, forged through both triumph and tragedy, make her a compassionate voice for families navigating whatever difficulties they face in this intricate tapestry called life.

Kathy and her husband live in Texas near their children and grandchildren.

Kathy would love to know you are reading this book. Please let us know how to pray for you in your journey: www.thekathyrogers. com/reading.

If you would like to have Kathy speak at your event, email info@ thekathyrogers.com.